WAR   LOVE

BY RAYVON PARKER

DISCLAIMER

I am only writing some of my own personal pains and or experiences regarding love and the hurt of being taken for granted. I speak of misunderstanding amongst people; sometimes misunderstandings that a simple conversation would fix. I speak of God's timing and overcoming adversity. All crime in this love story based on true events are entirely fictional to give the windy city situation some click-clack a thorough mfr in the street will appreciate. I'm not speaking on any specific incidents and or people, and anything regarding anyone other than myself is either coincidental or complete fiction.

ACKNOWLEDGEMENTS

First and most important: GOD IS GREAT!!!

Thank you God Almighty for shining your
     Grace on me. for your divine intervention
     Into my crazy life. for the many blessings!!!
     for the strength to make this all Happen.
     Next, i want to thank my mother Marva
     "Baybay" Parker and for birthing a Caesar!

     For providing me all that she gave enabling
her baby boy to stand on my own ten toes. next
thank you To my cousin the 'GODNELL' FOR
Financing Dirty130chicagobooks while I was
down and out, I LOVE YOU CUZIO!!!!!! Thanks to
my business partner and Little sister Stephanie
'supercharge' Harris For believing in me enough
to incorporate Our company dirty 130 Chicago
books LLC while i was locked in The belly of the
beast. putting Mad work in no matter her own
trials

     And tribulations. #FREEKINGMONEY my
younger brother Deonte 'King Money' Young
and Co-Owner of Dirty 130. that snake-rat gone
either get ate by a mongoose and or choke on
some bad cheese. You are coming home to a
empire lil bro FOREVER MY BROTHER, MY
BROTHER I LOVE 12-12 #AllHailKingDell

     Lawanna Welsh, I love you and appreciate
the powerful books you invested into for my re-
education, the selfless support. the love before
and after my reincarceration. Soul Sista you are
appreciated, selfless, and Heaven sent. Last yet

not least, my boi Leland 'LOCO' Jones shout out Welch for my boi. You gave me the notebook that birthed "War Love" so you got a chop Comin . i love you for being my prison therapist brody.To the supporters of Dirty 130 I love you all like I love me!!!!!

CHAPTER ONE

Did this Latino dude just nod his head at me?
BH thought.

As the jury were seated inside the jury box in the huge courtroom on 26th and California in Chicago Illinois. Although imperceptible to all except him and the Latino, BH returned the gesture.

"Has the jury reached a verdict?", asked the liver spotted evil ass lady judge.

"Yes, we have your honor." Responded the female foreman standing in front of her seat, inside the jury box with a scrap piece of paper clutched tightly in her small hands.

BH let his eyes wonder around the huge imposing courtroom and found it nearly empty. His trial had been rolling since earlier around twelve this afternoon. It was now nearing seven p.m. It didn't bother him that it took the jury under two hours to reach a verdict.

T-nator had shown his support with a brief pop in as well as K.C., Both big money men who had paid BH (big head) or Eujean (pronounced u-jean) to knock niggas dick in the dirt. No one expected and or believed he was coming home seeing as how he got jammed up.

Fifteen months ago...

BH and his man's Prince Capone had been leaving out of one of Prince drug spots in the hood, only to see a car full of suspicious looking shorties floating past. Upon closer inspection, BH recognized the front seat passenger as one of the main up and coming shooters for the other side. Prince had his head down fuckin around with his phone on either Facebook or Instagram.

"BH, on KD look at this dumb bitch. I ah- ", was as far as he got. BH drew his big chrome .40 Taurus and was in motion to dump all inside the lo-lo (cheap car) turtle nem was sliding in.

Before squeezing the trigger and putting the driver's brains on the windshield. and turtle's out the passenger window. that big head of his started to add shit up quick. Such as, why hadn't the little nigga turtle bailed out and attempted to jay down (shoot). And why were they fidgeting without looking in Prince and BH direction?

That's when the second car trailing them caught BH attention! The would-be killers lack of action all the sudden made perfect sense. 12! The police were locked in on turtle nem. And now they had a better target. BH wasn't going though.

Instead of fronting the trap off by running back inside knowing all had to have saw the cannon in his hand. he hit the gangway beside it and dashed across the alley to the next block. Surprisingly The unmarked crown Victoria had sped around and met him there. As the white officer leaped from the car, BH thought about squeezing that fat Taurus trigger and making his brave ass a hero.

He quickly nipped that thought in the bud and made an "about-face" the United States army would have been proud of. BH had on a navy blue Ferragamo shirt, Ferragamo belt, fitted navy blue true religion jeans and all white low top air force ones. *Ain't dressed for this shit*. BH thought as he ran for His freedom. He jumped a couple fences, wiped the chrome .40 down and was looking for somewhere to tuck it off as he heard an army of car doors opening and closing. This was followed by frantic chatter from they're handheld police radios, signaling the arrival of additional boys in blue.

noticing he was behind this bitch crib his brother fucked on. He smashed her back window in and tossed homer through before vaulting a couple more fences heading up the block. When he exited a cut on 57th Sangamon Street, it was possibly a hundred of Chicago's finest waiting on him.

"One more step and I will blow your fucking brains out!" An over eager police officer called out to BH with a cold yet hopeful glint in his eyes.

"Pull that trigger and I bet you lose a comrade every day this week my nigga." BH promised. He meant every word though he complied by raising both hands. BH was past crazy. Not stupid.

"My nigger?!" The white officer repeated irritably reaching for his handcuffs with one hand while still aiming his big bad policeman gun with the other. Point made. BH didn't have to say another word.

He was detained and roughly placed in the back of one of the many police cars that were parked out on the street. As they searched the immediate area for 'homer' (his chrome.40), he prayed they didn't hear that window shatter. Homer was filthy. He intended to get rid of it that day. The gang of police searched high and low well past eleven p.m., rolling right into shift change. He heard it in the excitement over the broadband police radio sitting in the front seat of the squad car.

"Found it!"

The same white officer that initiated the chase, walked over to the car flashing a beautiful chrome 9mm Beretta. BH could do nothing but laugh. Dirty ass CPD. Why wouldn't they have access to an unlimited number of untraceable guns in all makes, model, and color?

Without a doubt they had identified their runner by then. Eujean Fulton. Better known as big head the shoe collector (he hunted the steppas). Allegedly a reputed assassin. His criminal record resembled the fat bitch precious with Flava Flav on the side. He knew they thought they could lose him with this last case.

Especially with him being eligible for the armed habitual gun enhancement. In Illinois that was the equivalent to the California three strikes law, only for repeated gun offenders. BH is a thinker, a realist.

He knew there was a fifty-fifty percent chance that he'd get back or spend the next twenty years or so down and out with a thirty year prison sentence. He was twenty-four and it wasn't something he dwelled on seriously at that moment. He was adding up who all owed him money. Wasn't no bonding out no matter how many niggas with bags of money supporting him. He was released nine months ago from a stretch; he still had a year and change of parole time to complete.

Fast forward fifteen months...

The only spectators remaining in the courtroom was big heads fifty-one-year-old mother and his baby's mother Ameerah, whom is madly in love with him if she was left to tell it. He didn't fuck with her in any type of way. She was beyond beautiful on the outside but a straight thotiana. She kind of put you in the mind of Lisa ray in the movie player's club. Only thick as fuck and youthful at the age of twenty-two. He tried fuckin with her the long way, but she just wouldn't keep that pussy between him and her like the rubber band on a slingshot. He had yet to see the baby girl she swore on a stack of bibles is his. He refused all mail and visits from Ameerah. Not for the fact alone that he wasn't fuckin with her. BH couldn't fathom the thought of eujeana (pronounced u-jean-nah) being his and these dirty ass people putting him in a concrete Rubik's cube for the next thirty years. He knew unquestionably eujeana is his seed. Mom's duke stamped it, and she wouldn't hold no punches. She would have been kicked Ameerah to the curb. Baby named after him and all.

"Deputy, please." The liver spotted lady judge waved with a nonchalant flourish.

The sheriff's deputy stepped over to the jury box, accepted the folded piece of paper from the female foreman and passed it to the judge. The judge read the verdict quickly with disinterest before passing it back to the deputy and him to the jury.

"Mr. Fulton, please rise. Foreman, you may read your verdict. BH stood tall knowing he had got away with more shit than the former Chicago mayor Richard daily, however it came, it was his. He was handsome with his light brown skin and dreadlocks. Dressed in a Calvin Klein shirt patterned with small grey "ck" emblems all over it. Taylor made black Calvin Klein slacks, Ferragamo belt and Ferragamo loafers on his feet. the simple solid gold Cartier glasses he wore made him appear to be the intelligent person he was. With his hands clasped behind his back, Bh held his chin up for the blessing or bullshit.

"We the jury find the defendant Eujean Fulton, not guilty on count one of armed habitual   criminal.

We the jury find the defendant Eujean Fulton, not guilty on count two of uuw by a felon."

All BH could do is exhale the breath he'd been unconsciously holding. He got the 'B' he prayed for. By the grace of God, it wasn't his time to go. That's exactly what a heavy sentence following a conviction is; a chance to die breathing. Too many good men were entombed in those max joints and merely existed as zombies. The words "back down "was playing on repeat inside his head as his high-priced Irish lawyer Tim Bennett clapped him on the back.

"What I'd tell you Eujean? Did I earn a bonus or what? We'll talk about that after you get laid. Pussy Tends to make a man more generous." He laughed.

This dude nutty-butty, but I fuck wit em. BH thought happily. He nodded at his mom's duke, ignoring Ameerah blowing kisses at him as he was taken back to the holding pen to change into his brown cook county jail uniform. This was the part he hated. Walking all the way back to division 9 before being processed out.

When he hit the deck, all eyes landed on him. Most of them nervous. Those belonged to the few that rocked with BH. The ones who cared. The rest were mixed with the hoe ass niggas that prayed on the next man's down fall, and a couple that didn't care one way or the other.

BH threw both hands up flashing big pitchforks (GDN gang sign), then immediately started stacking hand grenades with a beaming smile. the whole 3c (tier he was housed) went wild.

"BH let me get that t-shirt!"

"Let me get the socks!"

"No homo, I want the boxers! I ain't wearin em tho."

"Bitch you gay askin for folks' boxers! I hope he got shit stains in em. I'm just fuckin wit you train. BH, rip the boxers in half!"

It was like that in division 9 of the cook county jail, everybody housed here was fighting drama: murder, attempted murder, home invasion, armed habitual criminal, armed robbery, etc. When a mafucka won their case at trial, niggas wanted a piece of that blessing. No matter what BH did in the streets, he acknowledged that higher power. There had to be a god.

"y'all know what it is First come first serve, Blessings to all you niggas!" BH said emotionally. Something he wasn't prone to feeling. He packed his personal papers, pictures, and mail. the c/o was back in no time to get him. He had a heavy heart leaving behind some good dudes.

Soon as he got to division 5 processing, he called one of his main men that was ironically from the other side.

"Moms told me already. Congrats bro, on stone."

"Hell yeah. What's the word over there?" BH inquired to make sure a caravan full of opps from the other side wasn't outside the county war ready.

"Nigga I'm out here, yo brother nem out here and Moesha thick ass out here in her Audi. She got your baby in her lap so pop out."

"Fa sho. they finna let us out now." BH said through a smile. "How this opp ass bitch know I'm Slidin?" BH wondered out loud. He stepped out the county and three familiar whips pulled up instantly. His man's G-law popped out his Impala and embraced him in a brotherly hug while his little brother stacks money was talking slick from the jeep Cherokee him and Pezzy were in.

"Big bro come on before we have to put this bitch on channel 9."

"Fasho." BH agreed. G-law grabbed his big bag of personal property and put it in the back seat of Moesha silver Audi, as he climbed into the passenger seat. Moesha is a dark brown skin super thick 4-foot 11-inch boogie bitch from the other side. She smiled at BH as he sat in the car. Braces shining like diamonds.

"Hey Eujean." (Pronounced u-jean)

"How yo phony ass know what's going on with me, huh?" He asked with mock aggression.

"Boy everybody know you beat your case. I called your momma too." She replied, laughing as she passed BH a .40 caliber smith and Wesson.

"Fa sho". He thanked her, gripping the almost compact black death bringer. "This G-law shit."

"Yeah. Ion know why his ass think he can give me guns and shit." She complained.

"aye, find somewhere to pull over real quick so I can fuck you in this car. " BH blurted abruptly. He was fuckin with her to see where her head was at.

She 'broke bad' on him (left him for dead in jail) after bumping into his young Westside chick. He really wasn't fuckin with her. She was a tool in his pursuit to catching that bag from now on. Nothing more, nothing less. With an itch for the sausage, she swerved the Audi. seriously looking for a place to park. Every spot she pointed out he shot down. He laughed from his kidneys the shit was so funny and told her to take him to his og crib.

"You want me to come up?" She asked hopefully, biting her bottom lip sexily.

"Naw. I gotta get all this county dirt off me. Ima call you in the mornin or some." He retrieved his bag filled with love, life and loyalty for the past 15 months from the back seat and stepped around to the back of his mom duke's apartment building in the foster park area. His right hand was in his right pants pocket gripping his new buddy.

CHAPTER TWO

"Get up, bitch! T- nator finna pull up." His brother money shouted, waking him from his peaceful sleep on their mother's couch.

"Fa sho." BH responded as he stretched the lingering sleep from his body before getting up to go into the one-bedroom apartments bathroom. After taking a piss, he finessed a shot of toothpaste out the nearly empty tube. Chasing it down with some Listerine mouthwash. All his gear was at Ro Ro house out west and he hadn't spoken to her since she bumped into Moesha. Ro-Ro cried about him making her look stupid and feeling played. At that time, BH was like man fuck you! Her! the clothes and everything else existing out in the free world. Bitch I'm facing 30 years for a gun these crooked ass Chicago police done put on me. if you won't understand that's where my attention at, ion need you.

As it stood, BH had nothing. Except the trial clothes and the smitty (smith and Wesson) G- law laid on him.

"Big Head, T-nator on his way up." Stacks called from the other side of the bathroom door.

Before he could respond, he heard a small baby start to cry. He immediately felt a strong emotion bloom in his corrupted chest all around where his heart should've been. A feeling like no other. Spitting the toothpaste and mouthwash mix out, he hurriedly rinsed his mouth and splashed water on his face. He shoved the sudden burst of nervous energy to the side stepping out the bathroom. He didn't even knock on his mother's bedroom door. Twisting the knob, BH walked right in. The room was dark, but he noticed a few silhouettes in his mother's queen size bed. Flipping the light on, he saw his moms duke still curled up sleep, and Ameerah rocking a beautiful butter pecan complexioned baby girl back and forth to quiet her. Ameerah's eyes were homed in onto BH. Admiring his short dreads, bulked up chest, and shoulders. Without procrastination he stepped inside the bedroom, over to the bed and lift the baby gently from Ameerah chest with sure hands, turning her around to face him. As God would bear witness, it was a love at first sight. When their identical dark brown eyes locked onto each other, BH and his baby girl smiled simultaneously.

"Daddy bwaybwee." BH offered in a funny little voice that even shocked him. Eujeana started to kick and reach for him happily." Damn Ameerah, I'm a father"

"Bruh, T-nator wanna rap with you really quick." His brother called from the livingroom.

"Aiight." BH replied stirring his mother's rest.

"Give me my baby Eujean." Ameerah said softly.

"Our baby. "He corrected, passing Eujeana back only for her to start acting up and reaching for him. When he picked her back up, she instantly went back into happy happy mode. BH put her close to his chest and stepped out his mother's room, closing the door behind him. The apartment was very small so stepping out the bedroom put him right in the front room.

"I knew Tim had that shit beat when he said, 'they thought they would sprinkle fairy dust on this gun and my clients' fingerprints would pop up.'" t-nator recounted and the three of them laughed.

"Yeah. Tim did his thang." BH said so to t-nator and thanked him for financing the heavy hitter attorney's expenses for him.

"No problem. You know I got y'all. Check this out though." He had a cloth Gucci bag carrying a large Gucci shoe box BH himself knew he couldn't fit. It being January in Chicago, he wore a big warm Canada goose coat. He came out his pocket with a thick brick of blue cheese secured with several rubber bands.

"that's supposed to be ten. That's fresh off the block so I don't know. I got some "C"(cocaine) for you two. I know you was locked in with Nick or you want some dog food (heroin)?"

"This good. The "C" too, that's love big bruh" BH said sincerely. Especially with a new nine-month-old baby girl.

"It ain't nothing." T-nator responded removing the Gucci shoe box from the bag. sitting it on the couch, Opening it to reveal four brand new pistols. A FNS 9mm-18 shot, p90 Ruger .45-15 shot, p89 roger 9 mm-17 shot and a p94 9mm-16 shot. Every slammer came with an extra clip and two boxes of ammo.

"These was waitin on you fifteen months ago. Stacks ran through a couple since then." This remark brought more laughter.

Eujeana was staring down into the box and started to reach for the dark metals. Solidifying she was daddy's little girl.

"Let me take ha bad butt in here wit them." BH said, excusing his self. He was back in a flash.

"Gone go shoppin and shit and get up with me later. We can slide to K.O.D (king of diamond) or something." T-nator said this clapping hands with BH and stacks.

"Fasho big bruh."

"I'm finna get in traffic wit T-nator big bro. "Henny weak pussy ass still got the wheel if you need traffic ..."

"Fasho." BH replied with the intention of spending quality time with his daughter. Henny is this red bone stacks Been fuckin with from the hood since all of them was Shorties. Her, BH, and stacks were so tight, ten times out of twelve, she was the behind the wheel when they stepped out and left a nigga shit on the curb. BH loved her like a real sister,but stacks was heartless. Sometimes, BH regretted taking his brothers training wheels off. The streets had been dripping red ever since from busted heads and broken hearts left in his younger brother's trail. After locking the front door behind his brother and T-nator, he played with his daughter for hours before he called his personal driver grime g (a GD from far over east) to come scoop Him to do some shopping. Grime was family. Drove his ass off. BH felt comfortable riding dirty with him. He gave his mom dukes $500 then gave Ameerah $500 and told her to spend it all on his baby. He

Ended up giving her another 500 to do something for herself. Though it wasn't in him to take care no hoe. she was the mother of his baby girl. He would make sure she was secured also. Grime g pulled up and they ended up at this high priced urban gear store called the shop. Rockstar Rockstar that. Timb. Mikes. Ones. He was Down two G's and change leaving the shop. But they had it on the gear. Since he was already on the east side, he went to grime g crib and got fly as fuck. It was time to network and see who needed who sent you know where -heaven or hell. If the real hustlers-maintained bags of money it would be somebody that wanted somebody else dead. BH's starting Price was $15000 a head. If it was already an opp $7500. From grime g phone he hit a few heavies. All let him know they would link with him later. Another thing that came natural to BH was extortion and all types of fuckery. First day out ain't even got his dick wet yet and was back to business. Grime was his Mans, but BH didn't work out his truck. He called henny and learned she was riding around with nothing to do.

"I'm finna pull up on you. let's slide out west",

"I'm wit it bro." She knew it was at least $500 in it for her if they were headed out there.

290 loved the brothers (BH and stacks money.)

****
******

"Big head what's up shorty". Two G, whom is the oldest brother of his ex- Ro Ro greeted him. They were on a block two g, Ro Ro, and they're brother Brandon controlled for the GD'S out on the Westside of Chicago. A lot of money came through this block right off division.

"Shit. Tryna see where the love at". BH replied, shakin up with two g.

"The love right here where it been. I told you to come out here and run yo bag up". He said while flagging his block runner over, "tell Ro Ro BH out here. Grab twenty-five hunnid and ten/fifteen of them hitters. BH, you want some pills too, right?"

"Whatever you blessin me wit. Much love Brody". BH said, whole time thinking about smacking ro-ro head off her shoulders.

"Fuck big head! Fuck big head! Fuck big head!" Roro bounced out of the two flat her and her brothers bought and put in auntie cat name before she passed away.

The only thing stopping BH from picking her little skinny chocolate ass up by her neck, was the Tears flowing down her beautiful face. Romeeka wasn't but nineteen and feisty as hell.

"Chill out wit that goofy ass emotional shit." Two G snapped at

His baby sister with a disgusted look on his face before walking back towards the t-alley and his lime green 71' Chevelle on 24-inch forgiatos.

"Eujean the goofy." She cried running up on him. "That bet not be that bitch BH! You bogus as hell! I shoulda never loved yo bogus ass."

BH wrapped his arms around her. Lifting her small frame with ease. And carried her inside the nicely remodeled two flats.

"Ro, you know what the fuck you said, Remember? 'BH we not together. Not until you leave the streets alone. Remember that?!" He rarely did anything without his aggression on level ten. Romeeka knew exactly how to make him flash out. And he did. Snatching her into that' you think you crazy zone where he done showed plenty they wasn't, both his hands now around her neck, weren't hurting her in the least no matter any outside perceptions. Yet they were tight enough with energy so hot his point landed on both feet; be cool.

"So what BH! It hurt me. Me! Me! Me! For her to feel like she could stand up in court for you. T - ", was as far as BH let her get. Fusing his lips with hers, he clamped her tongue between his teeth as it snaked over her lips and sucked on it the way he knew drove her. Drawing away with that young lust burning her limo tinted skin, she pulled him up the stairs and inside the apartment her and her brothers shared on the second floor. Into her bedroom they went.

She unbuttoned his Rockstar jeans before dipping down into a squat. Ro Ro was young yet suck and fuck she did better than most he knew. she was sucking slurping, and cursing the dick out all at the same dame time.

"Ooh... (slurp). I miss this. (kiss)...dick BH (slurp).

BH pulled her to her feet, and she unbuckled her Louis Vuitton belt and peeled her own pant off. Bending her over the queen-sized bed he was all too familiar with, he put the round came down. A quick hard fifteen months' worth that had his and hers cum running down the inside of her thighs. When he pulled out, she came up out of her shoes and pant. All lady prey or perish apparel. *some new shit BH Thought absent minded* as she licked him clean. Ro Ro left the room, returning a minute or two later with a wet warm towel and finished cleaning him up the right way. One thing BH always loved about her was how she took car herself better than women twice her age.

"I'm about to get in the shower, you might as well come on if you stayin." She offered with sassiness in Her tone. Ready to continue where they left off over Fifteen months ago. That all night loving she was used to with him wasn't happening though.

"Naw. I only popped out here to see where the love was at." BH said, tightening his belt.

"Right, her." She countered smartly, patting her little shaved pussy. BH only nodded his head up and down in agreement.

"We together now, right?"

"Come on ro. You left me for dead. We cool tho fasho, fa sho." BH responded honestly and peeped the fire about to re-ignite behind those chocolate brown eyes. Just as quickly, her face softened. "Fa sho, fa sho, huh? Get yo south side ass on then. I'm the one made yo crazy ass stop wearin them big ass shirts. Never thanked me for that tho." She said Teasingly.

"That's because I can't hide my big ass gun no more thanks to you." He said seriously and they both laughed.

"Eujean. Do you love anyone? yourself included?" Ro Ro asked randomly.

"fa sho, a lot of people. Romeeka included."

"Aww." Her sexy chocolate ass cooed and blushed, hugging him.

"don't get that pussy juice on these $600 pants. Wet em you bought em." BH joked. She slapped his arm.

"I got some for you before you leave." She walked Over to the closet and got a size 7 Nike shoe Box that he knew belonged to him. She opened the box and he saw three things that made him forgive her leaving him while he was locked up.

"Thought I spent yo lil money, didn't you? Un huh."

Three things; homer (the filthy chrome 40. Taurus)

The black diamond Ademar's Patek that he used homer on its owner's head literally a couple blocks over (still had its owners blood encrusted in between the diamonds). And three g's and change. He collected the money and left homer and the watch. It was probably smart she didn't try to get that off back then. That was a custom piece. The jewelry wasn't the reason he opened the stupid man's head up. Romeeka was. She was fucking with the dude prior to BH sliding between her legs. Ro Ro was a lady true blue if nothing else, even though dude was A heavy (nigga with big money) ro cut him off for a killer in a big shirt. In his feelings he caught Ro Ro on Madison shopping and slapped fire out that ass. that same night BH with his signature one shot, left his shit on the curb beside his Panamera. Porsche. He took his time collecting that time piece. Two for one. He gave the watch to Romeeka, and she cried her love and loyalty to him. Two G even consented to their union then. How could he not?

"Get rid of homer. That watch too. We can split that down the middle. Better know I fuck wit you longer than Halsted (a main street in Chicago-runs all the way through. Ro, I just don't wanna hurt you." This came from a heart he really didn't trust.

"I know big head. Be careful out here." She said before letting him out.

CHAPTER THREE

"BH threw up all on the side of my car and almost fell out the motherfucker on the expressway." Henny told them, laughing at BH.

They were at ihop getting it in. The night before they acted a fool at K.O.D to welcome BH home the right way. He gave henny a gee for taking him out west. That was one reason they were so tight. BH overlooked out for anybody he was in association with.

" You made me clean that shit up too. This morning" BH commented, eating his chicken enchilada. T-nator had unlimited bands in one dollar bills when they got to K.O.D., he handed all of them a gee (a thousand dollars-grand) to throw as soon as they Arrived. BH and henny both pocketed the thick bands of ones and were laughing about it now. A new addition to their circle, Pezzy baby mama yazzy was with them.

"y'all petty, I threw my g." She laughed.

"Yeah, and that's why Pezzy paying for y'all food out 'his pocket." BH cracked putting emphasizes 'his'.

"Stacks, baby I got us." Henny laughed louder pulling the thick wad of singles out her purse and BH cracked up.

"y'all embarrassin." Stacks said trying not to laugh.

"Yoo?" BH said, answering his phone.

"Get some wheels and get down here to the trump tower a-sap lil bruh." T- nator said, superheated.

"Fa sho." BH said, hanging up. Pezzy or henny. run me downtown real quick."

"I got yo bro." Henny offered. knowing it was crunch time.

"Bitch how you gone volunteer without askin me?" Stacks asked loudly. they already had the restaurants attention from being silly. This outburst from stacks really caught some ears.

"Money chill out. Pezzy come on." BH said defusing the situation but pezzy was shooting the side eye at his bm (baby mama).

"You good lil bro?" BH asked, Tryna figure stacks out. "I need traffic right now Brody"

"Gone head henny." His brother told her. Stacks was tired of henny. It was no hard feelings between him and his brother. She was irritating him and on top of that her pussy was super weak if he was left to tell it.

"Brody you know yo slice Comin." BH said honestly. He always cut his brother in after he did his thang solo.

Which was Appropriate since the traffic originated with him in the First place. BH and henny made it from oak lawn, to downtown in thirty minutes flat. They valet parked her 2015 Hyundai Electra and went up to t-nator penthouse. They were up there no more than twenty minutes And BH had his marching orders. He gave her the directions to where they were going and what was up. He didn't have to coach her when they got in the area of where he was finna do his thang. She knew. Turn the phones off and no matter what don't move the car.

"Hold on BH." Henny stopped him, jumping out the car after popping the trunk. Moments later she popped back in with one of her wigs, a tight leather jacket and a snap- back. He was instantly with it.

"Them people all around this motherfucker." She said with excitement. no fear present.

Removing his polo Ralph Lauren coat, he switched it with the tight leather jacket. He put her wig and snap- back on Gloved up already. he was suited and booted to rock and roll.

The compact .40 damn near fit snuggly in the jackets pocket. The fat little handle was the only part protruding. It was alright. His tight grip took care that. The hat shaded his face perfectly and that's all that mattered. This was a thirty thousand dollar move and he wanted this. Needed it. Climbing out the car, BH walked the two blocks over until he spotted the royal blue Lambo, suited arm and white hand on the steering wheel. He walked right up to the driver's side and knocked on the window with his left hand. like clock work the window slid down expectantly.

"Eujean, I didn't know Terrance was sending you-." His expression became perplexed as he started to take in the wig and tight jacket. Instinctively his eyes jerked with the movement of BH right hand. Forcing Tim head back slightly, BH jammed the smitty hard into the bridge of his European.

Boom!

His signature one shot and he let the 40. Smith and Wesson fall from his grip-into the lap of his former lawyer Tim Bennett. As the car parked immediately behind Tim's Lambo alarm started to go off, BH threw a switch in his walk as best he could and didn't second guess himself by looking back. He had blown one of the top lawyers in Chicago's brains out right on the side of the cook county courthouse.

T-nator let Tim believe someone was delivering a thirty-thousand-dollar cash bonus. For all the good work he'd done for the guys. Tim also represented two of the guys who got jammed (arrested) up with a bunch of guns and drugs in one of t - nator spots 'uptown' on the north-side (the pole where its cold).

The ignorant mafucka Tim was trying to coerce lil Kenny and toota to take a plea deal, where they give up

Their big boss man (that's the states attorneys' word). Tim knew this was t-nator. The man paying for his trusted services.

Lil Kenny had a visiting day early this morning and sent word to t-nator about what his lawyer advised him on what the best thing to do as his attorney. Therefore, BH is top in his field.

"That shit was loud as hell. "Henny said as BH got back in her car.

"Shoot back downtown, you just made five bands. What you finna go buy sis?" He said this so calmly, she laughed and screamed before driving off smoothly. As always.

"I fuckin love you brother."

"On big homie I love you more sus." BH replied sincerely, he locked slightly over four thousand in her arm rest Prior to leaving t-nator. He counted out and passed her four bands and told her she would get her remaining gee before they are left downtown. She was beyond appreciative and would've drove him around for free.

BH was a great person with a powerful aura. Secretly, henny wished it was him and not stacks she got in a Relationship with all of them years ago. They made it back down to the trump tower this time with BH going up by his self. He was back down in ten minutes flat with a small

Gucci backpack and a fifth of Remy xo. T-nator paid him forty thousand for being efficient.

The man BH was so cold at putting mafuckas to sleep, he was feared more so by the killers then the bag men. When big head the Shoe collector was on you it was a wrap.

He didn't care where he gave it to you, only that you had to have it.

It wasn't just business either, deep down BH knew every mafucka he killed no matter if he knew That person or not, it was personal. If God didn't will it, he didn't kill it. Straight like that. He wasn't a sendoff (lackey - fall guy) by far.

It was like this, take Tim for prime example. There wasn't a member of law enforcement in sight. He didn't See one on his way to do his thang nor when he was exiting stage left. God willed it so he killed it. Straight like that. Right next to one of the Busiest criminal court houses in the country.

They did a little shopping downtown then BH directed henny to take him on western street on the southwest side, where he dropped $5000 down on a 2017 BMW x6. All black with factory BMW wheels. To get caught fish bowling it (riding with clear glass windows) was detrimental to one's life in the city of Chicago. He went on Ashland Street And got the-limo tints applied professionally. Fully loaded, he got comfortable in the passenger seat. The wheel was henny's. It being later in the Day, they cruised the city sipping the xo after situating everything with the x6.

"This foreign lovely Brody. You Makin me wanna trade my lil baby in and get me one." Henny confessed as her phone rang. She had it connected to the car's Bluetooth playing "king diesel" featuring "pappy". Two Chicago artist that had the streets. "You have a prepaid call from Vanessa...Kendricks." An automated voice informed them.

"Damn. disconnect that for me." Henny said sucking on the blunt a few more times.

"Henny bitch, I'm fuckin locked up g." A familiar voice said once BH pressed one and put it on speaker.

"I see. Why tho?" Henny asked, confused.

"jr. Daddy. I ran him and this dirty ass bitch over he call his self-cheating on me wit."

"Girl yo ass is crazy." She responded, taking a sip of her drink. BH sat there quiet. Tryna recall where he heard that voice.

"I'm good g. This shit ain't nothing. I'm done wit him."

"When the fuck they lettin you out?!!"

"Girl my bond a hundred fuckin thousand. I need ten thousand to get out and I go back to court in two weeks." BH heard nothing except strength in her voice and he loved it.

"Damn." Was all henny could provide.

"I'm only worried about my babies henny. He know treasure not his, so he really been actin a fool. Soon I pushed her out and he saw that big ass head, I Knew she – ", henny hurried up and took the phone off speaker. That big head of his started to wonder.

"Henny who is that yo?" BH asked with undisguised aggression.

"My friend you kept callin schemer." His heart started to beat ferociously in his chest. He thought about shorty for a long time after their short time together. She disappeared on him Following the one night she was drunk and vented to him on how she was exhausted from the wear and tear the hurt from her son's father weighed. One thing led to another, and they did what grown folks do when they are feeling each other. They fucked. All night. When BH opened his eyes, schemer was gone.

Some real Cinderella shit.

"BH. Girl." She replied into her phone.

"Put it back on speaker g." BH told her with ice in his voice. She obeyed.

"Henny, I hope you ain't tell him shit." Shorty was saying.

"Tell me what Schemer? Matter fact. stand by the door, We finna come get you." He said seriously.

"don't play wit- "BH disconnected the call.

"Take me to get this bread henny. Don't say shit, I wanna hear it from her." That was BH. Quick to put two and two together to get his four.

"I swear to God! I'm sorry BH!" He waved her off dismissively.

He had fallen in love with Eujeana and the thought of becoming a father. The whole time, he was already A father. This was the first time he really wasn't feeling henny's presence.

When they pulled up to his og crib, he ran up through the back. Unlocking his small fireproof Safe, he quickly counted out ten thousand Majority in hundreds. put it in the Gucci bag and shot back down.

"Take the six and get her. come str8 back here henny." BH said before shooting back upstairs with the bottle of xo clutched tight.

CHAPTER FOUR... VANESSA

'This crazy ass nigga really bonded me out for ten thousand dollars.' Vanessa thought unbelievably as she walked out into the cold January weather without a coat. She had been comfortably warm in her truck when arrested.

She was looking for henny's diamond blue Hyundai Electra when the BMW x6 swerved up.

"Get in hoe." Henny snapped with real attitude.

"Damn bitch who dick you suckin?" Vanessa joked. whole time lusting over the luxurious vehicle as she got in the passenger seat.

"BH got this for him earlier."

"Awe. Drop me off at my momma crib." Vanessa said. Only happy to be free though she'd been locked up a day.

Her mind was on a hot bath and sleeping in her own bed with her babies.

"BH waitin on us Vanessa. I ain't never seen him Hurt. Bitch I was scared and that's my fuckin brother." Henny cried. Swiping a tear away as she sped down California street.

"Bitch you better slow down henny before you kill us yourself and he don't have to." Vanessa laughed. she was scared too but would never show it. BH name rang bells all over the city. Without a doubt a known killer. It wasn't her intentions to Sleep with him back in 2015.

Let alone get pregnant. She was going through It back then. Or rather jr. Daddy was putting her Through it. Henny threw a kick back (small party) and BH gave her an ear she never had in a man.

A street nigga at that. Great vibes and Hennessy Put you in the mood for some of the best sex and it's what they Had. Nothing more, nothing less.

Back home to her son's father she went.

Yeah.

She felt low for having to stoop to his level and Step out with another man. But then she found out she was pregnant. In a way, she knew it wasn't Jonathan's. She hoped it was. That a new baby would put them back on track.

Opposites attract though, right? It's like Johnathan put in overtime to hurt, mistreat, and overall do Vanessa wrong once he found out she Was with child again. Vanessa absorbed and reciprocated his bad energy; she did her best to miscarriage. She got extra sloppy drunk, high, and fought every bitch she knew or thought her baby daddy was fucking or looked at, she was past the term for an abortion, but felt. It was her duty to get rid of the baby, especially if it were Jonathan's.

God wouldn't let it happen. She gave birth to Treasure summer Taylor Anderson (she gave her Johnathan last name because she didn't know BH's. And she honestly wanted her family to work still). When she pushed her chocolate little princess out and Saw the huge boxed shaped head. She knew instantly who child treasure was.

Her one-night stand. When treasure opened her eyes for the first time, Vanessa saw those same browns she fell in love with drunk and all. She fell right in love with her baby girl.

The day she gave birth to her daughter was the day she asked God to bring BH back into their lives. To let him be a better man to her and her babies than jr., daddy. How did the saying go?

Better late than never? She knew she was wrong for not telling him. God willing. He would understand where she was stuck mentally and emotionally during her pregnancy. On top of That jr. Daddy was fucking her up physically. She had never been this small weight wise. All the stress. Heavy weed and liquor intake was taking its toll on her young body.

Henny and Vanessa pulled up not far actually from where she lived with her mother. Vanessa saw BH sitting on the back of henny Hyundai Electra with a

Bottle of Remy xo. He was dressed in a Rockstar blue jean out- fit. A pair of wheat timbs adorned his small size seven feet. The blue jean Rockstar jacket hugged his

Shoulders so perfectly, Vanessa squoze her in remembrance of their one-night stand.

"Girl call me later. I'm finna go in the house. This stuff y'all got goin on some lifetime drama shit and done blew my high anyway." henny cried, leaving the car running as she got out. Vanessa was more nervous than scared. She stayed

Seated in the heated passenger seat as she watched her best friend speak to BH.

Probably how sorry she is with Ha soft ass. Vanessa thought humorously. Henny then wrapped her arms tightly around his neck. BH returned the hug lightly with only one arm. Vanessa could tell they were extremely close, and she felt a stab of envy. Clutching his bottle, BH approached the driver's side of the BMW. With how aggressive he yanked the door open; she could tell he was drunk. On top of being angry.

What he said next surprised her.

"If you know how to drive, switch seats."

Vanessa got out of the passenger's side and left The door open as she went around the x6. When she Sat in the driver's seat, he closed the door softly behind her. This was the first time any man held a door for her. Her heart skipped a beat. As small as it may have seemed, that's what counted to a real woman.

"Take me to see my baby schemer." BH slurred from the passenger seat strapping his seat belt on.

"that's not my name. And no." she laughed. Not at what he said. For two other reasons.

1) at the nickname he had Given her when they first met. He claimed her shit was so different from what he was used to. So Aggressive. she had to be scheming on a mafucka.

2) She never met a man (a straight killer nonetheless) That put his seat belt on as soon as he entered a Car. He cared about his safety huh, she thought to herself. Mine too if he trusts me behind the wheel over his current state. Was her next thought.

"Fuck you mean, no?!"BH asked aggressively. Again, Vanessa had to squoze her thighs together. She was bleeding anyways. Everything BH said and did heat her body up, cat included.

"Yo ass been in jail the past fifteen months nigga. I been livin. I said no!" Vanessa snapped.

Yeah. BH was a bonafide killer. So was she, in more ways than one. Fear has never been a part of her repertoire. At least not towards life. For the well-being of her kids, but anything else, no. Hell Naw.

"Matter fact let me use yo phone or call me a cab. You not about to leave here drunk." she said, not knowing BH was too intelligent to ever let himself get drunk.

"G I'ma tell you one Mo time, take. Me. To. My baby." he reiterated this through clenched teeth.

"Let me get the fuck out this car. Nigga you don't scare me. I. Said. No!" She yelled, getting out the BMW.

Her mother lived ten to twelve blocks over. She had no problem walking. Coatless and all. That's exactly what she intended to do. She made it four blocks thinking the entire time; weak ass nigga wanted me to walk.

Skerrrt!

The Beemer cut off her path as she was

Finishing her thought. She was so caught up in her negative thinking, that all her concentration went to stopping her body from releasing its bladder. She was a milli - second from peeing on herself.

"Get in the car schemer." He said this with a sober tongue that made her double take.

As reckless as her tongue and attitude is, she walked around the car and placed her firm tired cheeks on his heated seats.

"I hate and love that walk. Keep walkin like that you gone make me kill ah mafucka. Where I'm goin'?" He asked staring her down, smiling from ear to ear at how crazy and sexy he is, she gave him her mother's address. He drove as if he had sense and got her home in under ten minutes. Pulling up in front her mother's house she really did not want to part ways with BH.

His energy was so raw and uncut, she wanted to wrap it around her like a blanket. Naw. All men are the same. Was the insecure thought she harbored. Only she didn't identify it as insecurity. Merely as wisdom from what she experienced for years.

"When you gone let see my baby G?" He asked civilly, the way a normal person should.

"Who said she was your baby?" Vanessa questioned in the same tone as his with her back pressed against the passenger's door.

"Gone head on G." BH dismissed her with barely controlled anger. Vanessa could tell she was pushing dangerous buttons. That he was ready to flash out. She wanted to reach over, turn the car off and take him by the hand to meet his chocolate twin. Instead, her nasty pride dominated.

"No problem. Thanks for bonding me out. "She said sarcastically with no real intention of opening up to him. It wasn't a game to her; she was the catch and he needed to do more than chase.

CHAPTER FIVE

The x6 had been parked for days. BH was Cooling it after giving Tim's Lamborghini a new interior design. A blood red lining. this wasn't his sole reason for being tucked off. He was investing as much time as God allowed with Eujeana. Granted, he couldn't get Vanessa and his mystery baby off his big head. BH smiled thinking back on Vanessa's call. Specifically, when she verbalized seeing the size of treasure head let her know who the father was. Eujeana inherited that same square, boxed shaped Head. If the procreation in question didn't have his box Shaped head, it wasn't his. Straight like that. T-nator called his phone to see if he wanted His base balls (ounces of cocaine) hard or soft. Soft Fa sho, was his response. It was established that nick would bring him a nine piece (nine ounces of cocaine) around five that day. BH cousin rude boi Nell moved soft with no problem. His boy prince Capone had a couple spots slamming.

So that work (drugs) was already moved.

Back to Business was all he thought, notably now there were two princesses he needed to be accountable for. He was starting to respect and love Meerah again. As a friend and mother to his Daughter though. Nothing more. She went out and got a job, said she was looking for them an apartment.

In her high hopes, 'them' was her, BH, and Eujeana. On clear view bright in BH's eyes, 'them' was her and somebody else. Eujeana was staying with daddy. Righteously with his pockets striving. he gave his og a thousand, and Ameerah a thousand to go shopping for themselves and Eujeana. BH also bought his moms a 2007 charger for the same price he leased the x6 for. With them absent, he was left in the crib by his lonely. A Few minutes past five, not long after nick dropped the work off. he got a call from henny.

"Hey brother. You still mad at me?" She asked timidly on cue when he answered.

"a lil bit but I still love yo stankin ass." He replied Honestly. Him and henny put a handful of mafuckas to sleep together, they're bond was in blood. Real life blood Brother and sister.

"You better. Especially if I'm finna get my ass beat for you. Where you at?"

"Ah mafucka beat yo ass they better be at peace. I'm steppin for mine fasho." BH vowed.

"Where you at brother?" Henny asked again and BH could tell she was smiling through the phone. It made him smile.

"Og crib. Wasn't Poppin out today. Wassup?"

"I'ma be there in twenty minutes. Get ready." She said and hung up.

BH jumped up off the couch and got in the shower. Dressing in another Rockstar outfit with a pair of navy-blue Jordan's. Hottest pair out that year and his favorite. 11's. He was ready to go when henny called. She was standing next to the x6, holding some colorful happy birthday bags when he came out the front of his mom duke's apartment building.

"Here." she said, tossing him her car keys. "Get them flowers off my back seat. I almost forgot em, give me yo key."

He did as she asked. He helped her load the back seat of his Beemer with all the gifts and flowers.

Then got in the passenger seat.

Not once did he question where they were going. Only when he saw they were across the way from his block on 56th where known killers hung, Did he grip the 18 shot FNS 9 mm he had tucked under his right leg. She drove into the snake turn (. Cul-de-sac on 56th shields) in order to turn the car around, before parking beside a nice small house. He saw a lot of activity going on inside through the big picture window when they first passed.

"Grab two of them bags and one of the flowers. they from you." Henny laughed. They walked up to the door of the small house, and it was instantly opened. Vanessa was glowing. Dark chocolate skin with a healthy tone. Similar dark browns only a shade lighter and her shape was crazy. On the outside, she was naturally beautiful. An inch or two taller than BH which was usually a turn off for him. Yet her aura reflected his. The entire 15 months he sat fighting For his life and the months before his arrest, this was the better half he felt calling out to his soul, she put the attitude on immediately.

"Really Henny?" Vanessa capped. BH sensed she was fronting and happy he was there with her friend. BH was smiling and had forgiven henny a hundred percent. She drew a line in the sand with this move.

"Wassup Schemer." BH spoke to Vanessa stepping inside the house.

"You know my name. Act like it before you get put out." Vanessa said, checkin BH. Whole time, no mafucka talked to him like that. That shit turned him on and made him respect her at the same time. She most definitely knew what was to him, like he knew off bat when one was pump-faking. She was the real deal Holyfield. He laughed.

"Aiight. Cool. Vanessa, where my baby?" He asked, seriously. Back to business.

"Upstairs in my granny bed sleep. We finna sing happy birthday to my og granny then I'ma take you up there." She responded staring deep into his eyes. To show him some respect and letting him know his presence was appreciated.

"Aiight Schemer." He smirked. She responded by poking her lips out and screwing her face up sexily.

He approached her granny alongside henny, passed her the gift bag and flowers and introduced himself as Eujean.

"I know who you are baby. Thank you." Og granny replied as she was accepting the bags and flowers from him. His Heart stopped as him and henny locked eyes.

"You treasure daddy. That baby a chocolate carbon copy of you boy." She clicked her tongue, laughing.

BH let out the breath he'd been holding In. Thinking She meant his street resume. His chest swelled with the confirmation of the matriarch of the family identifying his relation to his daughter.

Og granny opened half her gifts before they sung Happy birthday with BH standing behind Vanessa.

BH was Singing right along with everybody else. Henny and vanessa Were beyond surprised. They kept stealing looks at each other and laughing. BH didn't notice that he was the root of their humor.

He was feeling too good being able to be close Physically to the one he believed his soul locked onto.

He was so caught up in her aura that where he was and who he was, at that moment, didn't matter after they concluded singing happy birthday to vanessa og granny, the rest of the gifts were opened. Vanessa grabbed BH by the hand to lead him up the short flight of stairs. At the top, there were two bedrooms across from each other. Turning left, they entered a room full of females.

The group of women got quiet when BH and vanessa walked in. All eyes examining his face. Adding up his features, coming to the same conclusion as og granny.

BH lingered right inside the doorway while vanessa stepped over to the four-poster bed and picked up a sleeping baby girl. She turned back around to face him. Standing the baby on legs that were almost severely bowed, her feet pigeon toed same as her mothers. Squatting, BH reached out his hands in a come here Gesture. The baby girl looked up with his eyes, took two Painful steps and landed in his arms. His baby girl laid Her head on his heart. Right then BH promised his self He'd always be around in case his little princess needed to hear his heart beat strong, to know where the love was at.

"Treasure know who he is. Girl, she don't fuck wit nobody."

One of the females stated. Every other female present echoed her sentiments. Vanessa not so polite told them all to exit stage left. So, they could have some privacy.

"Damn, schemer...how you and henny gone keep part of me from me? What's wrong with her legs g?" BH asked, gently rubbing her tiny, bowed legs.

"Mine was the same way. Hers a lil worse. A doctor said she may need them broke so they can reconstruct themselves while she still a baby." She explained, ignoring the first part of his question purposely.

"Where the doctor so I can break his face. Ain't no mafucka breakin shit on my baby." BH spit.

Vanessa laughed. Knowing he meant every word.

"Why y'all keep her from me g?" He asked again.

"BH I was in a whole relationship for one. For two, you was supposed to be a revenge fuck. And three, you out here Killing people like it's some type of 9 to 5 with no remorse. Fuck outta here! I can do bad all by myself." She concluded confidently and firmly. He respected every point she made.

How could he Not? It was all valid. He did almost seven years straight before meeting her. He understood women a-lot Better now than he did in his teens, he only wished women took the time to bear witness to him being in a league all his own.

Authentic. Yeah. He stepped on heads like Italians Stepped on grapes. That didn't make him heartless.

He Was blessed with a heart of integrity. Dipped in gold and hand crafted by God when it came to the ones who loved him. His was an old soul. Ten toes down he stood beside his morals and principles with a genuineness like no other.

He verbalized all this to her right then and there. His baby girl was wide awake in his arms and attentive.

"You say all that hot shit now then turn out to be just like the last lame. I'm good on all that BH. You wanna be in her life, you get one chance." Vanessa gave him eye contact with every word.

"Do that chance come wit a plus two?" BH asked, confusing her.

"Plus two?!" She echoed; face twisted up. Ready to flash out.

"Plus two. You and lil man too. I'm pursuing. Everything about you different from what I'm used to, and I want it close by 24/7 – 365. And please stop sayin I kill people."

"BH! Seriously?!! Who don't know you kill people?! I been hearing yo name since I was a little girl runnin around on my tomboy shit. 'BH just killed so and so', 'BH just killed woo and woo." 'Like damn! Do BH ever play basketball or party?!" She said straight faced and they laughed hard. Treasure even felt the good vibe. To where she lifted her chin to look back at her smiling mommy. With a cute smile of her own, they conversed about how old treasure was 17 months.

What she ate or didn't eat. That she could barely walk before her legs started to hurt. About how old her son jr. Is. Repeating the same questions for him. He didn't have to question her wants. A Real man knows what a real woman wants, respect. Love, real love, honesty, protection and a significant other that could carry his own financially. Those were the basics which he had covered and then some. They were so deep in each other's conversation that only when og granny announce she was tired and put them out did they realize how late it was. Her son was with his daddy's people, which was rare.

She dressed treasure and asked BH could He dropped them off at home. Of course. He rode in the back, holding his daughter since they were without her cars seat. The whole ride, he was promising his Daughter the world. Telling her verbatim that he would kill anyone that hurt her, her mommy, or big brother. As henny pulled up to her mother's house, he didn't want to part with his baby, or her mother.

"Calm down BH. you gone see her again."
Vanessa assured him, unlocking her mother's
front door. She gave him her number. He called
her phone then and there so she would have
his.

"When?" He asked, not attempting to mask
his over eagerness to have involved them.

"Whenever you want. Just know soon you
play any games, you finished. I will call you
henny! She called over his shoulder and closed
the door behind her.

CHAPTER SIX...

"Why you give that hoe five bands?!" Stacks asked BH heated. They were in traffic with BH behind the wheel.

"I gave you ah nick too money. You tweakin lil bro." BH reminded him, sounding cooler than he felt. Henny should've gotten ten.

"that's my bitch. You give what you got for her to me and let me dish out what Ima dish out." Stacks vented. Sounding like a slick drunk ass pimp or something. "Not when she got that wheel for me. That's my rappy then. Yo bitch after. KC say that fat nigga from the other side got thirty on some. I'm finna slide and see what's up. Your wit it or what?" BH offered, changing the subject.

Back to business. He needed a crib out in the burbs or some.

His brother was moving in the opposite direction Figuratively and literally speaking. Fucking with a hundred plus thots that wasn't on a crumb. He knew the nigga was trickin off.

"Naw, do you big bro. 'D'(drop) me off at my bm crib."

"Which one?" BH asked looking over at his brother. He had six of em.

"Domo." He said in a tone as if BH should've known.

It was Gucci though. Domo lived in his path to the block. BH decided he wasn't breaking bread off this thirty. If his brother rather get dropped off with a broke bitch than check a fast easy bag, that was no mercy on his pockets. BH dropped his brother off and made his way to the block. He stopped at a gas station on 59th & Morgan To gas up the Beemer and get some swisher sweets. While he was at the counter paying for his Gas and blunts, he spotted a black 300 C with limo tints pull in off Morgan Street. It circled the lot, before pulling out onto the nine (59th) heading towards Halsted Street.

He saw two people in the front seats through the lighter tinted windshield, he couldn't see if Anybody was in the back. Macmoose, the Arab behind the counter, gave him two black bags and watched him situate the FNS 9 milli in the doubled-up bags.

Gripping the 18 shot busy boy (gun), he exited the G-station and went to pump his gas. His back was up Against the x6 so he could watch both entrances.

The $40 he put in the tank was going in slow as fuck, the first warning to him danger was near. It's crackin. He held the fns in his right hand while he pumped with his left.

As he was shaking the nozzle before removing it, he saw the bird brain with a white t-shirt tied around His head and face, creeping around the corner of the gas station with something slight gripped tight. BH aimed his gun over his head and gave the trigger two rapid taps.

Boom! Baw!

The would-be Taliban ducked back around the Corner as BH released the pump to dip around the Beamer. He was in. Calmly pulling out the gas station On the nine as the stupid motherfucker started to shoot at nothing.

Pop.pop.pop.pop.pop.pop.pop.

BH was already turning down his block when He heard what sounded like a. 380 going off. BH laughed. Everybody was shooters in 2017. Tearing mayor Richard

Emmanuel shit up. BH drove down to 572, stepping cut his car, he noticed the black bags were halfway up his arm. Both had exploded from the bottom.

I shoulda known. Kc remarked, shaking his head left to right. Here come them people (police). KC pointed Out.

KC and BH melted into one of the many houses secured for them on the block. BH wasn't aiming to hit the nigga. Only to give himself enough room to exit stage left. He wasn't Tryna make no movie that'll

Get him a fa sho life sentence. Kc called fool nem that ran the g-station upon hearing BH account of

Events. Macmoose told kc that their digital video recorder wasn't working when that situation happened. To thank BH for not putting their place of business on the five-o clock news.

They also let kc know the camera in back caught the dude slipping out a black 300 C. KC thank him and hung up the call.

"Who was that?" KC wondered, sitting in his seat at the card table with another heavy. And two original killers.

"Most likely dude nem from the other side." BH replied, shaking up with everyone at the table. Kc finished his game before waving BH into the kitchen.

"Yeah. Fatts got some on a shorty named Sydney from

Up in the seventies. Posed to have knocked his main gunner down bout a week ago."

"Ion kno em. You got the lo?" BH asked, ready to clear this smooth thirty. This would be his best year fa sho.

"Do I? Everything in this flip- (flip phone) pictures. Color car and address. Shorty new all got FNH 57s big head, come correct."

"You want ah chop stick (assault rifle)?!"

"Naw, where that fn57 you got?"

"In the car, I'm finna go get it now. That thirty secured on my name." He merched and left out to get the handgun choppa everybody in the country was going crazy for.

Shit. If dude nem had em, he was gone even the playing field. King Cobra came back with a prepaid Flip phone and a beige and black 21 shot FNH 57. BH chilled over there until the sun went downplaying cards for money. Once he felt the police was done beating the area down because of the incident earlier.

Blue tips (5.56 ammunition) on his hip, he was on the move. He called Henny and told her to meet him at the slot. Both promised they'd be there in twenty minutes. They met up at BH og crib with them getting in her Hyundai Electra.

"let's bend thru a few blocks. This my cousin nem shit."

She spoke. He had the FNH 57 and the FNS 9 which he passed to Henny.

"Yo cuzin don't know em? " She asked. knowing rude boi Nell was plugged from this area.

"Naw, but he know the nigga that got nailed (killed). He say it was ah mafucka he fuck wit, so I guess I'm doin cuzin a favor too." BH was in his zone.

Henny played their theme song by Yo Gotti. "9 x 9 is 81 I'm ah 90 babies born in 91." BH rapped, switching gotti bars to fit his year of birth instead. When they hit the nigga Sydney block, BH immediately saw the forest green challenger the nigga

Supposedly was riding. The block itself was dry though. As she drove pass the challenger on his passenger side, he strategically turned his entire Body towards Henny, passing her the blunt. This put her in a legitimate position to face him and eyeball the interior of the challenger.

"Its two boys in there!" She reported, excitedly.

"Spin the block." BH quarter backed as his phone started to ring. "Yo."

"Stand down big bro. That's my mans." Stacks money said into the phone when he answered.

"Where you at?" BH asked, thinking his brother already had the drop on Sydney.

"Just left the block. Finna slide in Sydney, meet me over there."

"I'm already over here. He sittin in ah green challenger right now. I got it." BH said, pointing out a spot for henny to park in on the next block.

"Big head that's our family you goofy ass dude!!!" Stacks yelled into the phone before disconnecting the call.

Ion know what this nigga talkin about. BH was beyond blew. His brother couldn't be serious.

"What he mean that's y'all family?" Henny asked, puzzled as well.

BH promised her ten thousand this round. She begged him to let her step- (kill). Dead fucking serious though! BH had

Doubled over with laughter because she wasn't pump-faking.

RAYVON PARKER   70

"Ion know g." He replied

That big head of his was drawing blanks at every turn on their family tree. Stacks money called him a few minutes later. It was a brief call. Stacks and pezzy slid Up in pezzy sort 8 jeep grand Cherokee. BH passed Henny A G and let her keep the FNS9 while he got in the Jeep with his brother nem. He told her to go enjoy Her night and be careful.

"Damn!" Pezzy laughed. "Big head bitch you almost stepped on Sydney"

"On big homie that shit ain't funny. "Said the mafucka who thought everything was funny. Pezzy said so.

"Bitch I know you ain't talkin." Pezzy laughed harder driving back around to the nigga Sydney block.

"What's up lil bro? That's 30k." BH said with patience.

"While yo was gone all of them years it was me and Lil Sydney big bro. That's our lil brother." Stacks stated Windy ass city couldn't be added up though. Can't put no price on love nor loyalty, only business. Got to know when to separate the two. BH did. He knew firsthand.

"What's the word then?" BH asked. The 30k erased from mental data base straight like that.

"We finna see now." They found a park and stepped up To the house the challenger was parked in front of.

A fat nigga gripping a mac 9 opened the door mac 11) up. BH hated to be in the presence of niggas he didn't know with guns in their hands.

"Dough go sit yo fat ass down wit that weak ass mac." Pezzy laughed, stepping inside the house.

" Yeah Aiight. We can jump right back in that jeep and

"You can take me to open this weak mafucka up right now." The fat dude said seriously to the wrong person.

"On my brother grave we gone. Pezzy accepted with no bluff to him. The fat dude left out right behind him.

No one attempted to stop them. BH and stacks went deeper into the house as one of the other guys went upstairs to get Sydney. When he came down BH noticed he was younger than stacks. Probably twenty to twenty-one.

Sydney sat on the fourth step from the bottom and tried to smile but failed.

"What's the word lil bruh." Stacks greeted him as they shook up. "This my big brother BH"

"I heard a lot about you big bruh." Sydney said. Trying that smile again. BH knew better. Shorty popped his cherry (Caught his first body). It was eating him up. The field wasn't for everybody. Nowadays it seemed as if no one understood that or cared.

"I saw em and start dumpin. Soon I saw all the blood, I knew." he stated in a tone automated on auto pilot. Yeah. Sydney was either gone do something real Stupid to jeopardize his life or a lot of mafuckas freedom. BH was ready to exit stage left. The entire House had a dark horrible energy choking the air. Sydney was mumbling something with his head down.

"Stack money! Wassup folks nem." this guy BH recognized called Down the stairs. Greeting his brother.

"Pistol!" Stacks smiled, and the name clicked.

"I was in mount sterling (prison) with you, my nigga." BH said. recalling where he knew him from.

"Big head Wassup my boy!" Pistol replied shaking up with BH. They were in the joint (penitentiary) together they were down they're putting the fear of God in niggas. Pistol was around BH age, if not the same. A certified Gangster. His energy was the only one semi balanced. BH could tell he was worried about having big head the bounty hunter in his crib with what they got going on right now.

"Money my blood lil brother my Brody, BH replied, seeing the question in pistol eyes.

"Sho is. You always talked about em. This lil mafucka my baby brother." Pistol said, playfully muffing Sydney's head.

Pistol knew how detrimental the time was after busting yo cherry in the field. Sydney either needed to kill again immediately or be watched and chaperoned very closely. When stacks busted his cherry, BH took him the same day and made him stand over a mafucka until it wasn't nothing left in the clip.

A thorough street nigga Couldn't take no chances. That shit was equivalent to when a woman gave birth and was diagnosed with post Partum stress disorder. Over a week had lapsed, but BH could tell pistol was keeping him close. They chopped it up for close to an hour. Pistol and Sydney were into it with their own guy. Things were beyond the sitting down point.Dude nem drew first blood when they killed Sydney And pistol older brother snow back in December. Christmas eve. Shot in the back of the head for reasons unknown to pistol and Sydney. It was believed to be over a brick of cocaine.

Snow was supposed to have made a play, but when the buyer asked for three bricks instead of one snow didn't take None with him. Pistol and Sydney said fuck letting it burn till it get confirmed like Meek rapped about In Tony's story. Snow was with the guys when he died, so it was on like a pair of socks.

"We on whatever y'all on. Look tho, the nigga Fatts got a big bag on Sydney. Money said.

BH almost drew his gun. Pistol shot a quick side eye at BH. Like he heard his thoughts. Right, there was a tear in the trust. Like a vet, pistol changed the subject smoothly. They chopped it up a little more before pezzy and the fat nigga came back, both eating Maxwell's.

BH had a bad feeling about the whole situation. Especially about his brother not having any tact.

CHAPTER SEVEN...VANESSA

"Ma please don't say nothing else to me. I'm tryin hard not to disrespect you." Vanessa said, trying to call henny again.

It was going on midnight. Valentine's day. And here she was bringing it in alone with her babies.

"Why the fuck is this bitch not answering?" Vanessa wondered out loud.

"I dare you to disrespect me in my house. Won't happen again!",

"Whatever ma, please!" She replied and treasure started to cry about her legs. When she looked at her daughters' sleepy brown eyes and big head, she caught herself smiling. She dialed BH number. Want you know, he answered on the second ring.

"Yoo." He said as usual.

"Can you please come get me and my kids?", she asked with her legs crossed at the ankles. Shaking.

"Where y'all at?" He asked. She heard him moving around on the other end of the phone. She told him and he let her know he was on his way.

Before hanging up he asked her were they alright!! No, they weren't. She would tell him when he got there. Not fifteen minutes later, he called to tell her he was on the porch. This nigga beat the jimmy johns commercial, damn! Vanessa thought happily.

"Here, get Treasure." Vanessa said, opening the door pointing at their baby strapped in her car seat.

BH picked up his daughter and took her out to the car while she got jr. And a couple bags. Her Mother came out on the porch talking crazy as they were strapping the kids in their seat belts.

"If the boy can post yo bail for being stupid. Make him Get y'all somewhere to live lil girl. You a lil girl and you always gone be a lil girl. No matter how many babies yo hot ass push out."

Vanessa didn't care what was on the radio. She turned it up to the max to drown her mother's words Out. Frustrated, she told him to take them to Henny crib.

She lived out in the suburbs. Obedient, he drove down 87th. Towards the Dan Ryan expressway. Turning the music down, he asked Vanessa what was wrong.

"My mama and her lazy, fat, weak ass husband always got some slick shit to say. I need to get my own shit."

Vanessa went on to vent that she was working at burger king yet didn't have anyone to watch the kids. Namely treasure with her being super anti-social. Even Towards her grandmother. On top of all her crying because she Didn't like nobody, treasure legs was constantly bothering her. No one wanted to put up with that. Jr's Daddy not helping in no form or fashion need no elaboration. She would be twenty- two in March, felt old, tired and used up already. For the life of her she couldn't understand what was so wrong with her.

"Naw g. You strong. Sexy. and yo energy is beyond beautiful. you gone be straight." he reassured her with confidence.

"I need a little help with the kids, and I can put us

Where we need to be." she stated. exposing her vulnerability When she didn't mean too.

She was tired of showing her Weaknesses to people that was supposed to care. For example: her mother. Sisters. and or jr. Daddy. For what? Them to say fuck her?

"Give me my one plus two and I promise not to drop the ball schemer." BH promised. On impulse, she reached over and played with his ear through his short locks, she loved the way he gave her his ear.

"I love yo ears BH. "She laughed sexily.

"If you could get a crib right now, where would it be? BH asked, cruising up the expressway.

"Anywhere out of Chicago. "She responded truthfully with a little sadness at the fact she didn't want to be in her hometown any longer. "But shit, while I'm here? Somewhere out here in the burbs until then."

"Get that out the armrest." he told her. She clicked the armrest open to see five rubber band stacks of twenties and fifties. Grabbing the money, she sat it onto his lap Thinking *'get yo stunting ass on.'* he picked the money up off his lap after a quick peek down and dropped it back in her lap.

"that's for you and our kids g. I'm here now." locking her eyes on his face. She knew. He was the one. It wasn't the money. It was. Not on no thirst trap gold digging shit.

This supposedly corroded heart, cold blooded killer. Selflessly came through for her and her kids back to Back effortlessly. She swore by God right then that she would never let anything happen to the good man with this lovely heart.

" BH, you gone be mine until they put both of us in a grave nigga you keep being you." she stated this with emotion she didn't know she still possessed after being hurt so many times. It scared her.

"Fa sho. I'm cool wit that too." he replied in by agreement.

Moments later. They were in Dolton, Illinois, pulling up at henny's crib. They couldn't see her car parked anywhere on the block. This prompted vanessa to call her repeatedly with henny not answering.

"Well. The hoe not answering." Vanessa surmised.

"Comfort suites right up the street. The kids sleep and its almost one in the morning get a room until tomorrow or however long you need it, I got you g."

"I'm not gettin no room unless you stayin wit us. Ain't no mafucka finna wrong turn me and my kids in no country club hills. "She said seriously with her legs crossed. This may have been the only time she has ever felt like a woman. This revelation was shocking to her. As her mother's words last night about her being a little girl rang true in her heart. Right beside the affection she was receiving from BH was showing. Her mother's words from an hour ago rang in her ears. "schemer you ain't ever gotta ask me twice to do anything for you and the kids. Only make sure it's what you really want. "BH said.

How do this nigga always say the right things? Vanessa asked herself.

" I want you BH. You can have yo one plus two. "she submitted and felt at ease doing so. With that he placed the car in drive.

" here. Keep the money. We together right?"

" fa sho. fa sho. Keep it tho. I be out and about. I may have to count on you one day. You feel me?"

She felt him and it gave chill bumps up and down both arms. He was saying if he was to get locked up or God forbids – killed. He wanted her in position already to continue to strive for them. They were at the hotel shortly after affirming their relationship status. Vanessa stuffed majority of the money in her purse, removing a few hundred for the room. He sat outside with the kids while she got a honeymoon suite. She got that room because it came with a Jacuzzi and California king size bed. That way all four of them would have some much needed leg room . She was still bleeding due to the birth control she was coming off of so wasn't no freaky stuff going down. If she remembered correctly (and she did) BH was a fucking freak! out of Gemini, what else did she expect?

She carried a heavy ass, sleeping jr. While BH Effortlessly carried treasure and they're few bags. They got the kids comfortable before vanessa went

In the bathroom with one of the bags to get in the shower. The whole-time showering, she was Praying and asking God to let this be the one. She had never felt this way.

It wasn't Financial satisfaction, nor sexual satisfaction that, Had her feeling warm all over in a world so cold. It was the genuine effort he was making to let her know with them is where he sincerely wanted to be.

Vanessa dried herself thoroughly before applying her lotion. When she came out the bathroom, for a split second, she Felt a stab of jealousy. BH was laying on the far-left side of the bed in his Nike jogging pants and a tank top. Treasure had come all the way across the bed and was sleeping peacefully with her big ass boxed shaped head on her daddy's chest. She calculated it for a split Second, then dismissed the thought.

Treasure had her daddy's head; wasn't no way they could share his chest no matter how muscled he was. Her leggings and baby doll belly shirt, she into the bed and snuggled up against him. She smiled at how perfectly she fit against his body as if it was as if its where she always belonged.

Vanessa woke up to a dozen roses and a giant heart Shaped box of chocolate. The kids were awake also and Eating breakfast platters from McDonald's on the Far side of the bed. BH was standing by the window with one hand in his jogging pant. The other holding his phone up to his ear.

Her phone was right next to her on the charger. Literally twenty something missed calls from henny And her mother flashed across the scene when she tapped it. Eyes half open. She pressed on henny number as she inhaled the fresh scent of The roses.

" Bitch you with my brother?" her best friend asked excitedly when she answered.

"Hoe if I was?" vanessa antagonized sleepily with a newly content smile.

" Do yo shit sus! Yo mama called me and gone say 'she had that killer come get her from my house late last night." henny fell out laughing and vanessa right along with her.

BH turned around and made his way over to the bed upon hearing vanessa laugh.

" That lady crazy." vanessa said focus on BH.

" Where y'all at?"

"On an island bitch. We didn't know where you was Last night so stop clockin where we at." vanessa joked snaking her neck, as if henny could see her.

" Bitches sho is throwin a lotta we we we we's like they

In France or sucked one last night." henny expertly countered. Swiftly from experience, vanessa side eyed the kids. Both of whom was looking for her smack dead in the face.

"You on speaker and the kids right here all in my face. Ima call you when I get up girl." vanessa said, disconnecting the call.

BH sat two more breakfast platters from McDonald's On the nightstand for her after warming them up in the Rooms microwave. She

RAYVON PARKER   86

wasn't trying to be picky, yet she didn't eat at McDonald's. She had been working at those type of restaurants too long.

" I'm good baby. Thank you for the flowers and for feeding them tho."

"Happy valentine's day beautiful. You don't gotta thank me for that."

"How long you get the room for?"

"Thank you. 3 days, why, you ready to leave me already." she cracked.

"I'ma have to be dead for you to leave me. What that tell You? "He countered possessively.

"That yo ass certified crazy and probably need a check."

"Been gettin one of those since I was a shorty."

They joked and talked all through her taking care of her hygiene. Finished with that. She washed the Kids up separate and got them dressed. She told BH he could drop them off at henny house if he had something to do.

He told her he wanted to go to chucky cheese. Which she later found out was jr. Idea.

Seeing as how treasures single word in her vocabulary was 'no', for some strange reason. They ended up at river oaks mall where Vanessa enjoyed a proper valentine's day breakfast at a ihop.

Next, BH took them shopping. Buying them all nice foam posite and Nike jogging outfits. jr. and BH matched. Her and treasure like wise.

The whole encounter was so surreal to vanessa. All of it.

Treasure's bond with her daddy was natural absent any artificial plays. It was as if BH and jr. shared the same blood too. With no shame, she found herself wishing it were so. Once they got to chucky cheese, the man made sure Treasure did everything she wanted to. Played every Game. While he damn near never broke a sweat. She not once cried about her legs hurting. Which is also a first. As a mother, she saw all when it came to her babies. Even when she wasn't looking. Like BH would rub and massage treasures legs gently As she played on the motorcycle game. Or have her kicking the balls all over the place. Even at vanessa! Jr. Was right beside them Every step of the way, while vanessa sat and ate pizza she didn't want to stop herself from smiling. She the moment to give thanks to God For finally sending her a real man and great father figure for her kids. Even if he did kill people for a living, overall, best valentine's day ever.

CHAPTER EIGHT

It had been a few weeks since BH got the job On Sydney. King cobra had been on his heels (Looking for him), who wouldn't be on his back when They got a twenty-thousand-dollar middleman fee hanging in the balance?

BH kept placating KC by telling him he was on top of it. His big head was working in over Drive. It was back on that 30k. In a whole new Way though. Fates was really a fucking opp from the other side that had a couple million buried in the hills.

BH knew for a fact he was funding a multitude of niggas that wanted him dead. He was a rock boy

(Rock boy for black stones was the equivalent to calling a Blood a slob) they were rock boys. He just also happen to be a brick layer (connect). Fatts parlayed everywhere ...

BH entertained the thought of linking Back up with pistol and Sydney, pour a bottle Of ketchup on shorty head, take some pictures with The flip to bait Fatts in, let him drop off the sack and they wrap him up for a half mil or better. This was all in that big head of his. He had been spending every free moment with his kids (jr. Included). Treasure adored her baby sister. Even though her little legs tended to give out fast, she pushed it a little further every time she was around eujeana. Wont you know, don't shit as sweet as what his big head was cooking up wouldn't ever go as planned? His phone rang while he was at the table breaking base balls (ounces of cocaine) off a raw half brick.

" Wassup money." he answered, balancing the phone with his shoulder up to his ear.

" Pezzy just got hit the fuck up big bruh. "His brother slurred.

Pezzy or TB was his rappy on a lot of hot shit. When he did the six and a half years straight, Him and pezzy were co-defendants on two high profile murders. TB had a robbery on the side that BH wasn't charged in. They were almost real blood brothers.

"Meerah, put this shit up."

"Where he at?" BH asked, dropping The coke on the mirror top table. He went in the bathroom as Meerah was coming out his mother's room and washed the residue from his hands.

"He got hit all in the neck and shit. He might not make it." stacks said, sounding high and drunk. It wasn't even one o clock in the afternoon yet.

"Money! Where pezzy at?!" BH was getting heated.

"The university. Yazzy say he in surgery. I ain't goin up there." BH heard him guzzling what sounded like liquor out of the bottle.

" I'm on my way." he ran out the door and was getting in his car when yazzy sent him a video link.

Standing next to the car, he watched as pistol and Pezzy walked in the barber shop on Ashland. Pezzy was all smiles until a giant nigga jumped out one of The chairs and fled towards the back off camera. A slightly chubby nigga in a chair right next to him Came from under his cape with two 's with sticks (extended clips) in em, opening on pezzy and pistol. Pezzy always taking the lead, caught practically everything the nigga was throwing. Pistol tried to throw a couple back from his FNH 57. Only the chubby nigga wouldn't let up. Pistol disappeared as the chubby nigga followed the giant mafucka. The video went black as he watched his best friend And brother bleed out. With tears storming down his face, he clicked on the video again and concentrated on the dig nigga and his shooter. He watched closely.

Fatts! The shooter had to be from the other side. BH thought. The way the nigga was throwing (shooting), BH knew him to be the real thang.

He knew the killers from the other side and Beyond. But knew he didn't know the nigga that got down on pezzy, what the fuck?

BH jumped in his Beemer with the FN on his lap And did his best to drive like he had some sense.

He prayed to God his mans didn't die, and he Promised the devil he'd get his blood times ten if he did.

Thirty minutes later, he was at the university. Pistol was already there. H could tell he had that FN 57 on him from the way he kept adjusting his pants. BH left his pole in the car. Wasn't nothing but twelve up there. Pezzy was still in surgery, had been for over an hour. Yazzy said they needed to fix a lung and Was now putting blood back into him. Pistol pulled him To the side. They were up there to get their hair cut when the nigga lil spider from his hood caught them lacking.

"Both niggas been tucked off BH. On snow grave we lacked hard." He said sadly.

"Where the nigga lil spider people at? Momma??Baby momma? Brother?! Sister?! Somebody finna die before I hear anything else bout pezzy." BH was unnaturally calm relaying this to pistol.

"He ain't got no mafucka. His momma died from cancer. Both his big brothers patched(dead). He get busy. It's just him." BH heard the uselessness grief supplied in pistol voice.

It made him feel useless.
RAYVON PARKER   93

Fuck it! He thought, slipping out the hospital. Pistol and

A few of his guys followed behind him. He told them find his brother for him. He was finna slide and make somebody momma cry hard tonight. The university was a hop, skip and a jump from the other side.

BH was two blocks away from where fatts family Lived. He checked his rearview mirror and froze . Not one, two car seats in the back, plus the numerous toys his kids left there, made him keeping going pass fatts block. This brought more tears . The old BH stayed ready to kill or lay his life for down" folks nem. All of the sudden he had a new agenda . Be here for his babies. And schemer . He was ready to propose.

Pezzy was dying though, the little red him on His left shoulder all but shouted at him . He bust a U-turn on Ashland and took the one way back towards fatts block. His phone choose now to glow and ring like never before .

He didn't intend on answering until he looked

Down and saw '1st in everything' flashing across the Screen. Schemer. His soul mate . If god didn't will it, He didn't kill it. He took his frustrations out on his steering wheel as he got from behind enemy lines.

Schemer wouldn't let up So he answered .

"Where you at BH? ", she asked worriedly.

"On my way to the hospital. where you at?", he asked calmly. Her voice, presence and love did that for him and he hadn't even touched or kissed the woman in almost two years.

"I'm at the hospital wet henny. Don't do nothing stupid baby Please?!" she begged and he knew then it was true. She was the one.

" I'm on my way."

****

Pistol and his whole gang were still on location when he Swerved back up a half hour later. Jazzy ran up on him crying.

"BH, he made it! He still here!" she cried, hugging him tightly. Yazzy recently gave birth to two beautiful twin boys for his mans. BH knew she was beyond thankful to God. Shamelessly, BH cried with her. Vanessa walked over and held ham while he blessed his soul of worries. "Schemer, I don't like these feelings. I was scared. Real life scared that I lost my nigga.

Then I just froze up ... I saw our kids' toys and the girls' seats, then you called ... " he was rushing his words out.

" Shush! It's okay BH. Ain't nothing wrong wit what you feel baby. It mean you got more to live for. God Tryna show you who else need you."

The doctor came out with pezzy blood covering his scrubs like in the movies and everything. It was with good news. Pezzy out hit fourteen times. The worst being one in and out his chest and back, collapsing a lung. The one in his neck was a flesh wound that was also in and out.

The nigga had been crucified. Both wrists. Both legs, Chest, stomach, and neck. Fourteen times. In and out. My boy was in critical but stable condition. That wasn't nothing except the grace of God, BH thought. Pezzy lost so much blood by the time they got him to the hospital. They were ready to pronounce him dead on arrival. The doctor claim he thought 'well if his heart beats long enough for us to get some blood in him, well try.'

"Your brother's heart was pumping similar to that of a stallion with literally no blood in his body. Never seen anything like it. God is good." the doctor Added straight like that, before stepping back through the doors he came out of.

Damn pezzy. After another hour of waiting, they mobbed they're way in to see him. Pezzy had close to fifty people who loved him surrounding his bed. Hospital security was terrified. It was probably twenty plus guns in that room. They called the police And everybody finally cleared out, touching pezzy toes or Fingers gently. My nigga loved out here. BH thought. Vanessa drove the x6 with BH in the passenger seat.

"Schemer, you wanna know what came to my mind earlier. "BH asked. FNH 57 under his leg, with his seat reclined.

"what's that?" she asked, looking over at him briefly, concentrating on driving.

"I still haven't tasted them sexy ass lips yet." BH said, biting down on his bottom lip.

"What you waitin on then?" she asked smartly, leaning over the armrest after she came to the next stop light.

When they locked lips and swapped tongues, they didn't come up for air until they heard horns blaring behind them. They both laughed. It was all love.

"Damn, schemer! Like in the movies g. Did you see the fireworks and everything too?" BH joked.

"Yeah baby. Fireworks and everything. They both laughed. As his phone started to ring.

"Yoo." BH said into his phone, seeing a number he didn't recognize.

"You at mom dukes' crib?" BH recognized g-law voice instantly.

" On the way to get my little ones from the area. Why? You Tryna flip me stone again?" BH asked playfully. This had been him and g-law routine for years. He was one of the few who visited him regularly while he was down all of them years.

"I need to. But look, fat boy dropped a dollar(100k) On you and 50 cent(50k) on lil bro. Posed to be another 50 on pezzy if he make it. Beware of the dogs (watch all killers)."

" I need fat boy lo (location)a-sap!" BH gritted. Adrenaline through the roof.

" Him, the nigga that got pezzy and a few more main pieces jumped on a plane to Miami a few hours ago. Right after that stunt."

" Damn g- law. I need something tonight."

" I'm yo brother, right? "g-law asked in his laid-back demeanor,

" Fa sho, fa sure."

" Aiight. Ima show you where the love at. Tell pezzy this for him tho. Later-law said. Ending the call.

Somewhere on the other side ...

G -law ended the call with BH before calling his cousin Poochy.

" Poochy, y'all still back there shootin dice?"

"On stone." He replied. G-law overheard the commotion in the background.

" tell shorty I got them Xd's he wanted. I'm finna pull up. He can step out now. I'm gone in five Moe." everything g-law did was silky smooth. No one knew much about his business. Back when his old man got sick and his og was only God knew where, momma Fulton took him and his baby brothers in. BH was a true friend and brother to him. He wasn't content with Greg (g-law) being quiet. He used to have g- law go up to Sherman

Park with him knowing the moes would get on dummy with him being a disciple. BH told glaw!

" If we fightin ten of these niggas at the same time, you gone learn how to fight or we gone keep getting beat."

He loved BH for them lessons. When his cousin Matthew was killed, BH blessed him with his first gun. A 40. smith and Wesson.

"I got it Greg. Give me the move." BH told him after g-law stood there like he was holding a poisoned snake.

" On stone I'm good g." that night with BH on his side all the way, he caught his first body avenging His cousin matt and killed an innocent bystander in the white castle on 55th and Ashland.

See, g- law and pezzy favored each other to a t. Back then, nine years ago, all pezzy and BH did was Hot shit. That big head was unmistakable. Witnesses swore on a stack of bibles a known it killer pezzy and big

Head that killed Dion and an innocent bystander.

Hence the murders they were charged with and fought for six years. G-law made sure they were Straight. Even tried to take the case. BH stopped him. Only the three knew who killed Dion and started this big war between the city (57th) and the other side (52nd). Love and loyalty.

G -law was sitting in a dark colored grand Am when turtle stepped out the cut with a. 380 in his hand.

" You gotta let me slide outta this & ball. On stone this bitch lo-key." turtle complimented, opening the Passenger door.

Boom!

G law never dropped his shark like smile as he knocked half of turtles face off. One shot, he had The little nigga brain matter all on the inside of the passenger door. Reaching over with gloved hands, he pulled the door closed before driving off calmly.

CHAPTER NINE... VANESSA

"Girl I'm finna Dec (decorate) this little house out. Vanessa said to henny. They were cleaning the 3-bedroom, 2-bathroom, basement And attic house out. Vanessa found " senior citizen couple, who Were private owners out in Hazel crest, Illinois. They Were selling their home for a hundred-five thousand. It even came with a two car garage the previous owner's son added as a gift to his parents. The best part is the owners would let them rent- to-own at twelve hundred Month following a ten thousand dollar down payment.

He Gave her that. BH gave her his whole safe. Her criminal case was dismissed also. A conversation BH orchestrated with Johnathan handled that. That ten thousand was on its way back in, in another three weeks.

He said he was done killing and was going to stop selling drugs once he paid for the house and stacked Enough to open a clothing store. Or something legit. His word to her were ' I'm retired from the streets." she would have to over- see their legit businesses. Is the stipulations agreed upon. Not a problem. She promised him. She didn't want to worry about him getting killed or locked up every time he left her and the kids.

She dropped him off at his cousin rude boi Nell house after getting the kids last night. When he got That phone call, he seemed like he'd recharged his anger. He let her take the car because she expected to get the keys to the house today.

"Schemer. Bitch that name fit yo ass perfectly. "Henny cracked from the kitchen where she was cleaning.

"What bitch?!" vanessa snapped, eyes wide, abandoning her task of mopping the dining room.

"Bond you out for ten thousand. Buy you a house. Give you My Beemer? What -,"

"Bitch! Yo Beemer?! I'm finna beat that ass." vanessa joked, swinging Mop water into the kitchen.

" Yes bitch! My brother first, my Beemer. Hoe he gone marry you next. Watch." henny stated observingly.

"tell me anything why don't you. "Vanessa replied.

"Bitch we ain't even fucked yet. He haven't tried again since the Hotel three weeks ago."

"Did the bleeding stop?" Henny asked from the kitchen. She knew how irregular coming off the birth control had her bleeding.

"Yeah. Yesterday. But then his friend got shot and somebody called and said some that made him mad again." Vanessa pouted.

"Calm down. How long before the furniture get here?"

 "Everything on the way now. I'm about to get my sister nem a uber so they can help. My uncle Sammy too."

"let's finish gettin the house together, put y'all bed together. Then we worry about yo hot ass pussy bitch." Henny Said and vanessa threw more mop water into the kitchen. They both laughed. The house was being filled with great energy as well as expensive furniture.

* * * **

"Bitch you bet not have spent all my brother money." Henny said commented. April, lucky, and vanessa uncle Sammy came and went.

They were sitting on the butter soft cream colored leather Sectional. A small, low oval glass coffee table sat in front of them with matching glass end tables on each side of the l' shaped sectional. A sixty-inch Samsung flat screen t.v. . hung over the fireplace. She laid a large Versace rug under the table that cost four thousand dollars alone. An eight Setting glass dining table was all that sat in the dining room while subzero oven, refrigerator fused with other name brand appliances adorned the kitchen .60" inch in their bedroom with a California king size bed. Cherry wood dresser and nightstand tables.

The kids Both had mahogany wood and 55" inch flat screen televisions hanging on their walls. There were two princess theme beds in the girl's room for Eujeana and treasure. All the walls were recently painted white. They left them that way. Vanessa didn't do anything to the basement. She planned to put a bar down there.

BH had over thirty thousand in his safe that sat at her mother's house until today. She spent what? - fourteen of that decorating their home. One thing he didn't do was trip about money. Especially when somebody was always giving him a thousand here. A thousand there. She knew it wasn't free money, niggas was paying to say they were connected or associated with the crazy killer. Extortion and all type of fuckery. Henny phone rang.

"Sus where you at?" Vanessa heard BH ask her friend.

"At yo new spot. Wassup?" She asked.

"Stay out the area for a minute. We might need to trade yo lil whip in too. Ima cover the difference. Vanessa snatched the phone from henny, but somebody else started to call her phone. Passing henny her phone, she called BH from hers.

"Where to big head ass at any way? Don't you wanna see yo new home?" She asked excitedly.

"Our new home. Send me some pictures." BH said, sounding distracted.

"You want pictures of the new bed too or you gone come see it in person?" She flirted, henny rolled her eyes and got up from the couch. Answering a call of her own.

"That do sound like my work." BH laughed. Talking to someone in his background. Right when she was about to flash out on his ass for not listening to her, he replied.

"I follow the rules of the road schemer. Ain't no runnin red lights for me. "She laughed hard. All the killing BH did, he was terrified of period pussy.

"Un un. The light been green or should I say pink since yesterday." She smiled, squeezing her legs together.

"Shit, in that case, come get me. You gotta come this way to get the kids anyway, right?"

"Yeah. You still wit yo cuzin?" She asked, jumping up to put her shoes on.

"Naw, we went back up to the hospital. The nigga pezzy think he superman. Wanna wake up talkin bout he hate hospitals.

"that's good. What happen? When the Comin home?" Henny said she was leaving. Vanessa barely noticed. She was caught up in her conversation with her man.

"They put his crazy ass in a medical induced coma so he could heal properly. I had some good news to give em, now we on our way back to rude boi Nell slot."

"Aiight babe. Thank God. I'm finna be on my way." Vanessa's phone rang as she disconnected from BH.

She saw that it was her big sister the kids were with her down at og granny.

"Wassup bitch! My kids driven y'all crazy! "She half joked leaving out the house.

"Girl where henny?!" lucky inquired too geeked.

"She left in her car about 15 minutes ago. Why?" Vanessa asked, getting in the x6 and pulling off.

"They sayin BH killed the boy turtle last night out her car. Now it supposed to be money on the head. Him and her." Lucky gossiped.

"What?!" Vanessa screamed, slamming on the brakes. It kind of made sense with BH calling a while ago offering to buy henny a new car. "Who told you this?!"

"Shay shay from the other side supposed to have saw it happen"

"Let me call this girl." Hanging up on her sister she tried to call henny repeatedly with no success.

She kept calling as she made her way to Dolton. Hoping her best friend was headed the same way. Not getting an answer from henny, she called BH .

"Yoo, you outside?" He picked up on the first ring, excitement apparent in his voice.

"What the fuck? I asked you not to do no dumb shit BH. Now they sayin its money on you and-," click!

BH hung up on her. The phone was going straight to voicemail every time she dialed back. Throwing her phone in the passenger seat, she pressed down harder on the gas.

Somewhere on the other side …. a half hour later.

"Come out." Henny told lil dip.

Yeah. He was an opp (enemy). But she went to school with Him and been fucking on him for years. He called her while she was at vanessa and BH house. Begging her to slide on him. Vanessa with all her freaky talk with BH made her horny. If she wasn't gone, get hers. Stacks was acting like he had the only dick out south. A bitch as her had to prove him wrong.

Henny felt she had been in front lil dip house To get him after she got the kids. Make him wait.

All that had taken an hour, now he wanted to call! That was when her phone rang like crazy.

"Hello?" She spoke. Answering for lucky.

"They got henny!" Lucky cried on face time.

Vanessa stomach Dropped.

RAYVON PARKER   111

"Who? Please don't do this to my god!" vanessa cried, pulling over to the side of the road. BH started face timing her then. She hung up on her sister to answer for him.

"Vanessa where the fuck you at yo?!!!" He yelled at her. She could tell he was mad as hell.

"What happen to Desiree (henny) BH? What happen??" She bawled thinking the worse.

"We sent a lawyer up there. She good. Come get me from Nell crib now!" He said, hanging up. She was confused.

CHAPTER TEN

BH sat in the passenger seat of his x6 beyond pissed the fuck off. How stupid could henny be? He Specifically told her to stay out the area, warned her the car was hot. He never liked talking over the phone about anything halfway illegal. Yeah, he got word of him and henny names being thrown under the bus. For that, he would see the lil hoe shay shay. Henny was at the university now too. Broke left arm and a fractured left leg. The dead nigga ripped out two tennis ball sized knots of her hair. That's what the dumb bitch get. BH thought. He loved henny and knew he was happy she was breathing. But damn, her pussy on top of stupidity could have cost him or his brother their life.

T-nator sent a top-notch criminal defense attorney to the hospital to represent her. BH was the first Person henny told them to contact when she regained consciousness from the crash. She was being questioned about the dead guy and the gun in her lap. Once the lawyer arrived, she recounted to the best of her ability for the police, what happen. She was meeting a friend when one guy (Darius -lil dip) she knew

From high school. Approached her placing a gun to her head with one hand. He grabbed her hair with the other while demanding she get out of her car. She attempted to drive off and he tried to shoot her. Fortunately, she was able to wrestle the gun away, and shoot him instead, defending herself as his friends recklessly tried to kill her. Nothing else she could recall prior to the crash. And Or blacking out. The lawyer said the tearing out of her hair are defensive wounds.

The deceased brain matter found in the back of henny hair, tied in with the bullet holes in her Wrecked vehicle corroborated her story. clean and cut justifiable homicide. She was blessed to be alive and free to go.

The bitch was kissed on her bald spots by God fa sho, fa sho. BH mused, shaking his head. He did something he wasn't prone to doing. He confided in vanessa that his mans (no name was given) stepped on turtle. On his bloodline, him and henny nor her car had anything to do with that move.

He was drunk and high and spent a night over rude boi Nell crib. He hung up on her before she could say too much. He was trying to call henny his self when he got the call from the hospital about her situation.

"BH, whatever you got goin on is gettin closer and closer to home. Make sure we are secured baby.

"You, our kids, and me." She stated emotionally as they arrived home.

"Fa sho my queen." He promised. In two days, two of the closest people to him had been touched.

Nodding his head in understanding, he got out the car and vanessa followed. He grabbed treasure while she got jr. They couldn't see henny until the morning. She was doped up. Besides, visiting hours were over.

"You did yo mafuckin thang baby. Look at this shit." BH said, playing with the electrical blinds like a little kid.

"Thank you. 'we' did our thang. Henny, lucky, and April helped. Uncle Sammy too, I gave everybody a hundred dollars. Vanessa informed him walking into their bedroom behind.

"Come here schemer." BH said, they had laid the kids in their beds. He couldn't wait to tear that ass up. Vanessa stepped right into his arms. He palmed both cheeks firmly as she offered him her tongue.

"BH, I love you." She moaned.

"I love you more."

"I love you more. "Vanessa echoed.

"I love you infinitely then." BH said, picking her up by the back of her thighs and laying her on the California king sized bed.

"And I love you more than all that." She affirmed.

BH was high on pure lust. He paused.

"Hold up. Ima get in the shower real quick." BH said, starting to rise off her. She locked her legs around his waist and lowered him back on top of her. The heat between them at that moment Could have been used to make a full course meal.

"Permission to bring the streets in our bed this one time. I'm clean and you ain't no dirty nigga." Vanessa whispered, biting his bottom lip.

She pulled his shirt over his head and the rest of Their clothes were gone in a flash. BH didn't eat pussy at all. Yet he couldn't resist at least kissing her lower lips too. Sliding down between her legs, intending to kiss the cat only. Turned into a thirty-minute conversation. Her Lil clit started to jump, and he accepted the challenge. Tongue versus clit, she cheated when a slight squirt Shot out and he had to lick her clean. Vanessa yanked him back up, licked his lips clean of her juices while she gripped his dick with one hand, balls the other and guided him slowly inside her.

> Their love is so raw, it made the sex Phenomenal. With every thrust, their souls and hearts sent electric currents back and forth. Both stayed busy. Real love is what they went three rounds making. Fucking. Boning. with a lot of licking on each other Until exhausted.

Eventually they Fell asleep wrapped up together like a warm pretzel.

****

BH woke up the next morning to the bed empty, and The house smelling real breakfast like. He got up and into the shower in his own home.

It made him feel Like a real man for the first time in his adult life. To top it off he finally had a real woman to Lay beside him and wake up to. He wanted this forever and he knew it.

BH went downstairs and Into a room full of love. The stairs were right off the dining room. Vanessa had the table resembling something off the t.v.; beautiful.

"Fuck you cookin for? the clumps?" he asked, only semi playing. Vanessa laughed from the kitchen.

"Wake the kids up and Ima show you the clumps."

BH went in jr. Room first and wrestled him up Onto his feet. Then he went and got his little princess. He woke her and made her leapfrog down the stairs and up to the dining room table. She laughed the entire ride.

They sat at the table as a real family should with jr. To his left and treasure at Vanessa's right.

They ate good. No pork! Grapes and sliced bananas. Apple and orange juice. Turkey bacon, turkey sausage, chocolate chip pan cake's, cheese eggs and toast.

One little person missing. Eujeana. He gave Ameerah five bands since she was making the effort To do something for herself. She was the mother of his baby girl. He would make sure she didn't struggle neither.

She bought a nice little car and got an apartment in Indiana. He told her the minute a nigga moved in with her, he was gettin eujeana and would cease to help her financially. He needed to go out west (west side of Chicago) in a minute.

Ro ro got rid of the watch for 50k. They were splitting that. He needed the 25 k. Especially following the down payment on the house, plus furnishing it. Schemer enjoyed the x6 so much, he planned on surprising her with one of her own. Her birthday was in two weeks. Most likely it would be then.

"Thank you, schemer. This food is so good." BH complimented around a mouthful of eggs.

"Who is see -Mer?" Jr. Asked innocently and they all laughed.

"Thank your big head. You welcome." Vanessa said.

"Big head!" Treasure repeated and every one's mouths dropped open. Treasure covered her mouth to stifle her tiny giggles.

"Say it again mommy." Vanessa encouraged standing from her seat and squatting on the side of treasures highchair.

Treasure shook her head no. Giggling and trying to stop more eggs from falling out her mouth.

"Treasure got a big head! Treasure got a big head!" BH

Started to chant. Jr. And vanessa caught on and chanted along with him.

"No! Big head!" Treasure laughed, pointing at BH.

To vanessa and BH, this was equivalent to her saying 'Daddy.' all of them had the surprised look on them Face again. Treasure started to choke on her eggs, she was laughing so hard. Vanessa snatched her out of her highchair and pat her back until she calmed. Once treasure was safe from choking, she immediately said:

"Big head!", pointing at her daddy.

"Ima show you the big head." BH teased, springing from his seat at the table. Leave my baby alone! Vanessa screamed playfully, running around the Table with a gleeful treasure.

"Ahh!" Jr yelled out in surprise as BH ejected him from his seat at the table. Placing him on top of his head as he continued to chase vanessa and treasure all through the house. They all ended up in vanessa and BH bedroom having a royal rumble on the expansive bed. BH won after tickling everybody into submission. Vanessa turned on a kid movie that they watched as a family.

"What time visiting hours at the university start?" Vanessa asked a dozing BH.

"What time is it now?"

"11:27."

"11:00. I need you to take me to get a rental quick." BH said, getting up out the bed.

"Okay. Let me get the kids together. Vanessa replied getting up with him.

BH went in the safe and took four bands out. He put on a prey or perish apparel shirt that had a severed hand On the front, holding a double cup with a cross melting through the bottom. Percocet and Xan's overflowing over the top. And rock star pants, with a pair of mikes (Jordan's) on his feet.

"That shirt so fuckin raw and I like how them pants look on you. Turn around." Vanessa toad BH while combing her long had into a bun. He turned around and kicked the safe closed.

"Its two bands on the bed for you. Take one of them poles (guns) too. The smallest one."

"Already did. I got the biggest one. The grey one." She smiled at him walking out the bedroom. She had grabbed the p90 rouger .45.

"that's cool too. I need to get some fast." BH said, coming down the stairs. "low-key tho."

They left the house deciding on enterprise, where she talked him Into a red Camaro. He rented it for a week. He asked her if she wanted to take the Camaro. She laughed at him. Speeding off in the BMW. He sped straight out west. The Camaro was a beast! He opened 290 expressway up doing 130 easy.

Abruptly he decreased the speed when he thought about how big money pops died in the 300 with the hemi in it. Division and ridgeway was live as usual. Ro ro had a new Lexus truck she was sitting in. BH materialized right up next to her.

"Yo big head ass almost got shot. "She joked climbing out her truck with a big MGM book bag.

"With what, yo finger?" He capped back as she got in.

"I heard yo baby mama look like me?" She smirked, applying lip gloss.

"Better. "He replied, seriously. Roro cut her eyes at him sharply. When she saw he was dead ass, she reopened the car door.

"Say thank you for the bag at least." She slammed the door without giving him a chance to respond. He smashed off down to the other end of the block. He held no kick it tickets for anyone but his schemer no way. He chopped it up with two-g nem for a few minutes. There was no way he was finna ride around with 25k and play chicken ass (a goofy). He merged onto the e-way and did a hundred all the way back to the burbs.

"Yoo." He said into his phone, seeing his brother face timing him.

"Damn bitch. Fuck you drivin that sound like that?" Stacks

Asked. BH flipped the camera around to show him the Camaro dash and red hood.

"Bring that mafucka this way."

"Aiight. I'm on my way to the slot real fast, where you at?" BH asked slowing down to get off at his exit.

"Domo crib." Stacks said, cheesing. BH shook his head in the negative. 50k on his head, and he was still entertaining his chicken head ass baby mama.

"Aiight. Give me twenty minutes in this bitch." BH predicted, disconnecting the call.

Arriving home, he saw the x6 parked in front the garage. He backed in next to it. Snatching the bag up, he stepped in the house. It was his intention to be in and out. When he walked inside the bedroom, vanessa was sleeping. Naked. Fat chocolate cheeks facing him with a super fat pink pussy sandwich sitting between her thighs. Dropping the bag on the floor. He pimped over to the bed and tried to put a hickey right on her pearl. The pussy was his.

"Ooh. Ahhh...BH." She moaned sleepily. He flipped her over on her back and sucked the pussy with vigor. Eagerly, he went for broke and licked around that butt hole. She was into its fa sho, fa sho. Alternating from rubbing her pussy and ass on his tongue.

He loved how she tasted. He put one finger in her butt while he sucked on her clit until it swelled.

When he put one finger in her pussy also and challenged her clit to a duel, she did that lil squirt thing and he cleaned his plate.

"Hurry up and get in the shower." Vanessa ordered him breathlessly. She didn't have to tell him twice. His shower was the matrix. He was in and out like at the carwash.

When he walked back in the bedroom, his shit was on brick. Nine inches of steel.

"Come here." She beckoned him from the bed, best believe he stepped up, and she performed. Had him perched on the tip of his toes, desperately trying to run. He didn't wanna give her his nut like this. Hesitantly he stopped her, kissing her lips which were still puckered. Spinning her around, he saw firsthand the pussy was swollen And soaking wet. Seemingly steaming and inviting from the nut he had her squirting.

"BH!" She moaned, wiggling her hips subjectively. Her pussy was so beautiful it should have been in a museum. He was in a trance.

He slid in slowly while she arched her back to accommodate him. Immediately he knew he'd lied to her. How could I not kill again? Bh thought. Vanessa pussy was to kill or die for. This is his. The universe knew it. It better. These thoughts consumed him as he was one with his lady.

His queen. He dove all the way into the depths of her until She cried out, he let the tip of his dick knock on the bottom gently. Consistent. Suddenly, slowly he retreated. Watching the cream from her overflowing pot coat his long-handled spoon. He needed to taste her again.

"no. No ..." She whined like an aroused lioness at the brief 6 of physical contact as his dick plopped out of her audible. Hungrily he attacked her with his mouth again. He sucked

RAYVON PARKER   126

the juices out the pussy and licked the butt so good she was shaking, crying and begging him to fuck her in either hole. She didn't care if he filled her back up and tore her back up. (That he did.) Back on top of her, he pounded the pussy until she was screaming 'you bet not fuck nobody else like this' and laying prone.

"I'm cumin!" She cried with the sheet bawled in her fist and

It made him explode in her.

"don't make me kill no mafucka over you schemer." He said emotionally, falling asleep.

CHAPTER ELEVEN...VANESSA

"BH! Get yo ass up!"

She woke up two hours ago to take a shower and tripped over his mgm bag. Knowing it was money or clothes, she picked it up to either put it in the laundry basket or the safe. Opening the bag, she could've pissed herself.

The book bag was full of money. Five dollar Bills and up. This wasn't the movies, and she was Without a money counting machine.

It took her more Then two hours to count fifty thousand dollars in what was obviously block (drug) money.

"Yoo." He said turning over with a satisfied smile on his face.

"Where yo big head ass get all this money from?" She asked, hoping he didn't rob drug dealers as a side hustle from killing people.

"How much is it? You better know how to count." He joked making her snatch the pillow from under his head.

"Fifty thousand dollars." She replied. "I know I'm gettin a car for my birthday now."

"Stop pokin them lips out like that. That's 25k. Smart ass can't even eyeball count huh." He said, thinking he was right.

"If it's more than twenty- five, can I have the extra's?" She asked sweetly, really believing he Robbed somebody since he didn't even know how much it was.

"Let me see." BH said, sitting up in the bed after hearing the seriousness in her voice.

"See." Vanessa said throwing fifty re-rubber banded stacks at him.

"Hold up." BH grabbed his phone off the nightstand with A confused look on his face. "a ro. You know that bag had a whole fifty in it?"

"I said say thank you. "Vanessa heard a female voice say on the other end of the phone before hanging up on BH.

The look of admiration that crossed his face is what made her hot with jealousy.

"Who was that?" Vanessa questioned quietly and it shocked her.

Her usual attitude was tamed at the thought of another being able to please him so easily.

"My ex -." He responded honesty. It only made her hotter.

"Remember what you said when you came in me? Before you went to sleep?" She asked in the same quiet tone.

"Yeah." He nodded.

"Practice what you preach and don't make me kill a bitch over you." She flashed out with her usual attitude. Vanessa jumped up to go take her shower.

She wanted To cry but wouldn't. I hope this is not the start of the dumb shit. Vanessa prayed aloud standing under the shower spray.

"Ahhh!" She screamed as BH popped out of nowhere and started to dump the money in the bathtub on her feet.

"You can have all that shit. All the money in the world can't buy you love and all the love in the world went earn you trust."

"BH!" She exclaimed shocked, turning the shower off Quickly. He had walked out the bathroom already.

"BH come get this money!" She called out but he didn't respond.

She wasn't touching that shit. A lot of dirt was running down the drain off it.

Vanessa Got out the shower to make BH come get the money out the tub and saw that he was gone. She picked up her phone and face timed him.

"Yoo." Answered, she could tell he was speeding.

"First off, slow down." She said and could visibly see the Car slowing.

"Second, where you goin?"

"To get my lil brother."

"I thought we was goin to see henny nem. That's why I dropped the kids off wit my momma."

"I'ma meet you up there. I posed to went got him three hours ago. That red snapper between yo legs put a nigga down." BH admitted dreamily.

She smiled brightly at him and mentally pat herself on the back.

"Flattery gets you a freaky treat so keep Poppin that good shit." Vanessa said encouragingly.

"Yo pussy so good it taste like god feet - umm umm good." BH Sang and she fell out laughing.

"You gettin corny baby." She stated good natured.

"that's what a great woman ah do to a Killa. Make him Wanna be a cornball." He replied lovingly.

"I love you BH."

"I love you more schemer.

"I love you more." Vanessa echoed.

"I love you infinitely." BH said.

"And I love you more than all that." Vanessa promised.

"I can tell." BH responded, hanging up.

Like a little girl, she was blushing with butterfly's fluttering in her stomach. Using her blow dryer, she dried the money best she could and just threw some towels over it. Leaving it in the bathtub.

She dried off thoroughly before oiling her skin up and Getting dressed. She put on a lady prey or perish shirt That hosted a pair of nicely shaped severed women legs With the word carnivore across the chest. And a pair of yell jeans and her foam posit nike's. She was on Her way to see henny.

* * *

"Desiree, you got a body under to belt." Vanessa highlighted for henny and herself unbelievably. This provoked more tears from henny.

"God was with you girl. I was prayin so hard when lucky told me that shit." Vanessa cried with her.

"a lie. Dumb bitch was fuckin on lil dip too, mad hoe. Ima do that slut worse than I did him." Henny threatened as BH, and stacks walked in with t-nator.

"yooo." BH fake shouted through cuffed hands. Him and t-nator walked over to embrace her. Both being mindful of her injuries. Stacks posted up next to the door mugging her best friend.

"Ugg! Don't look at me!" Henny sniffled, dipping her head under the cover to hide her bandaged bald spots with her free hand.

"You good lil sus. A rider for sure. Here, got some for you." T-nator said, handing her a small Gucci clutch.

"Thank you big bruh." She spoke.

"Open it." He encouraged. When she did, all saw it was full of crisp one-hundred-dollar bills.

"that's ten towards you a new car." T-nator said.

"Thank you." She cried. A tall skinny boy slipped in the room with a red Kansas City fitted cap on with his hands tucked in a red matching Kansas City pull over hoody. For a second vanessa thought it was BH friend pezzy.

"g -law Wassup Brody." BH greeted him with genuine happiness. The boy g -law said something quietly to BH, who nodded. Stepping over to henny bedside, he removed a big bundle

RAYVON PARKER   134

of money out of his pocket and passed it to her. Right then, vanessa grasped how important her best friend is in the streets.

"that's 10k sus. Towards you a new car. My apologies for what you went through." G-law apologized, leaving the hospital room as smoothly as he'd came. Vanessa knew intuitively that he was the one killed the boy turtle.

"Well, I guess I can keep my twos and few." BH said and all of them laughed. Stacks still hadn't spoken one word.

"You want half? Henny asked. Everyone knew she was talking to stacks. He looked around the room quickly, before chuckling darkly. It gave vanessa chills.

"Much love lil sus. Let's let them talk schemer." BH said.

T-nator stepped out prior to the boy g-law coming in. BH. Handed stacks the keys to the Camaro and told him he would see him later. Vanessa wanted to ask henny was she comfortable having twenty thousand dollars in a hospital bed with her. She didn't want to offend BH or his evil acting brother though.

Let's no to red lobster BH. I love they shrimp. Vanessa pouted, knowing he loved to see her lips poked out.

Let's go. He responded. They got in the car and vanessa wanted to know what was up with his brother.

"What you mean?" BH asked. Not with talking about anyone outside of that person's presence. Even his own brother.

"Why he act evil? Like, your energy glow good and warm. And his just cold." BH laughed.

"Maybe it was just cold in that hospital room." BH said, laughing harder at the don't play with me mafucka look she threw him.

"Naw. My lil brother been thru a lot with the females. Ion know what else to tell you. He harmless tho." BH said, laughing again. Vanessa was serious. Henny was her best friend.

She got enough going on with mafuckas literally trying to kill her. Then the way henny asked him did he want half her money as if stacks was her pimp or some.

I mean, he didn't even seem like he cared that she was laying there with broken bones. Whatever though. Vanesa was done with the

RAYVON PARKER   136

conversation. He got one pass since he was her daughters uncle and future husband brother.

They made it to red lobster and enjoyed a feast. Ate so much shrimp and crab legs, their stomach & were About to burst. They made sure to get the kids some crab legs and shrimp also. Treasure and jr. ate everything mommy and daddy ate. It was time to go and get them red lobster. They were parking in front of Vanessa's mother house when BH received a face time call from stacks.

"Where you at big bro?" Vanessa could hear stacks was crying and it shocked her.

"Gettin the kids. Why Wassup?" BH asked sitting up in his seat.

"Sidney shot his self in front of the momma big bro. He gone. Dead big bro." Stacks was emotional. It made vanessa feel bad about how she was talking about him a little over an hour ago.

"Damn.", was all BH said in response.

"His body still in the house. I'm over here now. Big bro he shot his self-wit that same move. "Stacks said, vanessa didn't know what he meant.

"Dammmn." BH exclaimed drawing it out. Obviously, he knew exactly what his brother was saying. "They gone tie em together. Damn."

"You finna pull up?" Stacks asked hopefully. Right then, he sounded like a little boy lost.

"Naw. Shit, ain't nothing I can do. You need to move around, ain't No tellin what type of investigators out over there. From the Streets or police." BH responded, being the thinker he is, vanessa was looking down at stacks face and could tell he didn't take it as a pull up and he verbalized it.

"On big homie ion give no fuck who out here. That's my lil brother, I ah die behind him!"

"Money, he gone! Shot his self! Fuck is wrong wit you? Go get put up and call me in the a.m. (morning). "BH flashed out and stacks hung up on him " fuck is wrong wit this nigga."

"Sound like he need his big brother, you sure you don't wanna go over there for a minute?" Vanessa asked seeing things from the outside / in.

"Hell Naw!" BH snapped at her. "I knew that shit was gone happen. Shorty drunk that red drink without guidance. Then killed his self wit the gun he killed another mafucka wit and everybody know. On top of all that, me Nigga pezzy all fucked up behind this shit, what you say schemer? This situation gettin too close to home. I'm puttin a cap on it. Point blank. Period. Like you said."

"Okay BH. I'm sorry." She apologized.

"Sorry for what schemer? You ain't did or said nothing wrong. I'm just tired of this shit. Ain't none of it worth it. They hit one of ours. We hit one of theirs. Now the title of the shit they killed folks now it's bussin, fuck that." BH expressed with heavy emotion.

"I'ma see if my momma will keep the kids tonight." Vanessa said reaching for her phone.

"Naw g. I need our babies bright energy. Yo bright energy around me as much as possible." He said, stopping her. Her heart swelled. Matter fact, we goin to get gee gee (Eujeana) tonight too."

CHAPTER TWELVE

BH hadn't spoken to his brother in over a week. This was his first time seeing him at Sydney's funeral.

The only reason BH was present was due to his hot ass homie pezzy leaving the hospital so he could be there. Pezzy couldn't even walk on his own yet with all the times he had been hit in both legs. The nigga had pins everywhere. It didn't stop him from tucking a p89 rouger with a stick (extended clip) in it, up under his leg.

BH pushed pezzy wheelchair and watched his younger brother carry Sydney casket. Pistol p was fucked up. Both his blood brothers was gone. Leaving their mothers middle child here alone.

BH felt for him. No doubt. It was why he was ready to walk away while he still got his only brother,

His life, and his freedom. He killed thirteen mafuckas in his young twenty- six years on this earth. Four of those were murder for hire.

The other nine! Love and loyalty. To what end though? For whatever lasting satisfaction when

He couldn't even remember the first nigga he killed. He didn't want to remember. the game was the game in Chicago. The only thing changing was the names and faces of the players, killers and drug dealers, he wasn't sticking around to see a lil BH. No way no how.

It was a black cloud over the whole service, same as the day BH, pezzy, and stacks went over to the house. BH believed every nigga in attendance was poled up. He forbade henny and vanessa from coming cause shit didn't feel right with the whole situation. From start to present time. It was a trend in Chicago for the opps to come shoot up a mafucka funeral.

What better way to catch a mafucka lacking? BH himself had a FNH 57 full of blue tips on

His hip. For niggas to play crazy at Sydney funeral. Pistol led the pall barriers to Sydney plot. Carefully they placed his all white with gold trimming Casket over his plot and a few words were said. You Could tell a lot of funerals had been going on. It Was more mud then grass with banquets of flowers All over the cemetery. After they lowered Sydney into the ground, everybody dropped their roses into his grave and the cemetery started to clear out.

"BH lets slide on lil spider." Pezzy said after BH helped him into the passenger seat.

"In what, yo wheelchair? "BH countered seriously, placing pezzy wheelchair in the back.

This had become his family's ride, pezzy was tweaking.

"On my brother grave don't do that to me. That nigga painted Ashland (main street on Chicago's South side) with my blood." pezzy reminded him with hostility.

"Not in this pezzy. Ima get the maro if that's what you really wanna do." BH stated getting behind the wheel Of the X6.

Merch(swear)it." Pezzy challenged. still hot.

"On big homie." BH merched it.

"Aiight big head bitch. Call money." BH paid

for the rental for another two weeks

When his brother stop answering his phone. Ain't no Telling what type of moves done been made in the Camaro, BH rather it be that whip then the X6, he could always report it stolen and move with that alibi.

He just didn't need to have twelve on him for

No weak meat ball ass shit. They ended up t in the Wild hundreds at a spot pistol secured. That's where Sydney's repast was held.

Everybody besides BH was highly Intoxicated. Pezzy included. Though he knew damn well He wasn't supposed to be drinking.

"21-gun salute! All nines!!!", pezzy yelled out drunk. On his Jada kiss shit.

Rolling his chair toward the back yard, ten to fifteen niggas followed him. all brandishing guns. BH went and sat in his car as probably twenty drunk ass niggas start letting off shots in the air.

Boom boom boom ....

Boc. Boc Boc boc ....

Pop. Pop. Pop. Pop. Pop. Pop. Pop.

CPD was nowhere in sight. That shit sounded ridiculous! Unreal! Niggas was letting Off full clips. not a few shots. Schemer chose then to face time him.

"Yoo." He answered while the shots were still going off practically right next to him.

"What the fuck! BH?" She screamed and he smiled.

"I'm on my way home." BH said as the shooting stopped on cue.

"BH what is goin on?" She asked worriedly.

"These niggas drunk. I'm finna drop pezzy off. Then come home to y'all."

"Hurry up. My pussy need to be licked and kissed. My butt too." Vanessa purred sexily holding the camera on her wet fat pussy.

"You gone get pezzy left. Let me go get this nigga." BH said dead ass climbing out his car.

"Hurry up BH." Vanessa repeated sexily with a close of pretty pussy.

When BH walked inside the gate surrounding The front of the house, police cars started to come from every direction. All dirty mafuckas (niggas with guns and or drugs) dipped into the house. BH followed them passing his FNH 57 to dough and left back out to find pezzy. Walking around to the back, he saw man's empty wheelchair. He took his phone out to call pezzy. no answer. Walking back around to the front pushing pezzy wheelchair.

He saw the front door to the house had been closed and locked. The police were in the yard, knocking on the door with guns drawn!

"Let me see your hands!" A police officer demanded with his gun aimed at BH head. He complied raising both hands.

"Do you live here sir? Any id?" Another officer asked.

"This is the place! There is a shit load of casings in the backyard." One officer stated, returning from the back flashlight in hand.

"Sir. Do you have any identification on you?"

"Yeah. In my left front pocket." BH responded. The cooler he was the quicker he could exit stage left. His phone started to ring. Letting him know somebody was trying to face time him, as one of the officers were patting him down.

With his hands raised, he couldn't Answer. His phone rang again as another officer was returning his id to him. The officer with his id whispered something to a plain clothed officer who simply nodded. He was told he was free to leave. BH walked over to his Beemer and got in. The plain clothed officer came over and knocked on his window. His phone rang again this time he took it out his pocket and saw it was vanessa. He answered while lowering the window halfway at the same time.

"You mind if I search the car?"

"Yeah, I mind. No, you cannot search my car officer." BH replied respectfully. "Wassup baby?"

"what's goin on now?" Vanessa asked. She got out the bed snatching any clothes in sight.

"I do not consent to a search officer. Is there anything else?" BH asked respectfully as he started his car.

"Why don't you want the car searched? Guns or drugs? Step out of the vehicle sir. "The officer said reaching for his gun.

"Oh my god Eujean. I'm callin yo momma." Vanessa cried. Probably thinking he had done some or was Dirty. He texted her t-nator number and told her to call him too. Also, that he was clean. Then he got out the car with his hands up. He was hand cuffed and detained on the curb while they searched his car illegally. After thirty minutes or so of them pulling and pushing, he was uncuffed and told to go home. From vanessa. His Mom dukes, Ameerah, t-nator. And an unknown number. Driving off, he face timed his lady.

"Thank god, come home now BH." She said worriedly. "I'm not hanging up neither. just come home."

He sat on FaceTime with her until he pulled up in front of their home. BH was tired. vanessa was standing with the front door open, dressed in a short silk kimono robe.

BH wrapped his arms around her waist
Breathing her natural fragrance in.
Moving his hands lower he gripped her
big firm ass. Letting experienced fingers
on both hands tease separate holes.

"I told you they need to be kissed and
licked." She moaned.

"You want me to suck on this pretty lil pussy
huh?" BH asked in between their tongue
wrestling.

"Un huh." Vanessa mumbled around his
tongue. He brought his left hand around to
tease her clit with his thumb. They kissed,
exploring each other's bodies all the way to the
bedroom. BH phone started to ring an inch or so
from the bed. Looking down he saw it was from
that unknown number.

"Yo." He answered, intending to be brief.
Especially since schemer had his dick gripped in
both hands. Rubbing it

On her fat wet pussy. He always answered
his phone.

He Remembered the times he needed a
mafucka to pick up his call-in life-threatening
situations and it

Didn't happen.

"g, you still out?"

"Literally just made it in." BH replied, it was g-law.

"Fat boy back in town. I been around him for half the day. He paid for a double funeral for lil Moe nem."

G-law informed him. That adrenaline shot he loved and hated woke him right back up. Unconsciously, he separated his self from vanessa.

"Please tell me you around him now?!" BH asked with his fingers Crossed.

"Right now. We on the station. He out here in his Bentley. Get here now. Ima clear the way."

Opps headquarters on the other side ...

"911, yes, my name is James stems. I'm a 69year-old, 25-year homeowner. There are a crowd of young men outside my home being loud and unruly. I believe I saw a gun or two." Glaw said from his white impala into his phone. He gave them the address to Fat's father house as his residence before hanging up. G-law was a ghost. He was well respected throughout the other side because He was considered a square in the eyes of the moes. One Who worked a job at fed ex. G-law seemed to be able to come up on an unlimited number of guns and made sure the moes had them. G-law was black stone to the bone, yet blood didn't make you family all the time. Genuine love and Loyalty did. No one on this green earth was closer to him then big head. His friend and brother. Whom Helped him avenge his cousin. then selflessly took the murder charges for him.

He would get out the car right now and blow fatts brains out himself if that was what BH wanted him to do . BH already proved he'd kill or die breathing (do a life sentence) for G-Law. Where BH stood he definitely knew where the love was at . g-law was tempted to pop out his impala and take this for his brother.

It wasn't a lot of the moes still out. It was going on one in the morning. Everybody was leaving . Tired or too high to keep the police showed up four car deep. Moe nem that were armed, cleared out while fatts with a neck and both wrists full of jewels was the distraction. G-law placed his personal 40. smith and Wesson on his hip.

He was licensed to carry concealed. Fatts and everyone Knew this . Another plus why the Moe's loved g-law . He would come through in times like this and secure the brothers. Most of the time his intention was to secure the nation.

 Not this night . He was securing family. It was what it was, and what it wasn't it'll never be. Fatts saw G-law and his eyes lit up. The address y'all giving is my address officer . Here go mi id my name is James stems Jr,."

"Okay sir. we see that. you guys keep it down though. It's the wee hours of the morning." One police officer stated. Handing Fatts his ID Back. With that the police cars We're leaving.

 "You got to shit on you Moe?" Fatts asked with poorly hidden fear and anxiety.

"Yes, sir law. here." G-law took his forty out the holster on his hip and tried to pass it to Fatts. Knowing he wouldn't take it.

"Yo aim better than my stone. Stay right here wit me. Ima get outta here in a couple of em." He smiled. sweating profusely.

"Aiight, let me turn my car off." G-law said. excusing his self as he saw two figures turn the corner coming from the boulevard on 55". Fatts saw them also.

"Aye Moe." He started. "Never mind." He spoke. seeing that it was most likely two clucks (crack heads).

One of them, the man with two children chairs. one in each hand. And a woman. With long wild hair flowing all over her head. carrying it look like a big bottle of bleach in one hand. They had that crack head bop to em.

"Damn! I thought that was big head nem." G-law said aloud. Ducked off in his car. He watched the woman Set the bleach down and come out the inside of Her bubble coat with a boomerang. (don't know why but Those were his thoughts initially) and spray Fatts fathers

Full porch one of the moes with a two-hand grip.

Baw. Baw, Baw Baw. Baw. Baw. Baw.

Fatts froze up against his Bentley. The nigga upped a boomerang himself (now known to be guns with extended clips). Ran up and shot Fatts in the face point blank range!

Boom!

Whole time while Fatts is being assassinated, shorty was still spraying the houses down on crowd control.

Baw. Baw, Baw, Baw, Baw, Baw.

Big head! G-law smiled that shark like smile Of his as he watched BH wrap his hand around every Chain laying on Fat's chest and drag it over his Busted head. They both raced back towards 55th With big head throwin (shooting) rapidly down the block.

Boom! Boom! Boom! Boom! Boom!

Boom!

This was g-law cue. Jumping out his car, he ran behind BH nem shooting over their head.

Boc ... Bloc... Boc ... Boc.

BH and the female spun and threw back at him!!

Boom! Boom!

Baw Baw Baw!

G - law ducked behind a car as a couple more of the Moe's popped out with guns. All of them started to shoot

In the general direction of 55th. Police sirens could be heard gettin nearer. So, vice new hit the gang ways and disappeared. G-Law walked over to Fatts and saw even in death, with the back of his head missing. He looked terrified and was sweating harder.

CHAPTER THIRTEEN

"BH you not takin that shit in my house." Vanessa flashed out on him as she pulled up in front of their home. She was referring to the chains he took off the dead man's neck. BH balled the front of his hoody up around the jewelry before he got in the car. *That shit had that man blood and brains in it!*

The thought made her shiver.

"Aiight vanessa. Go in the house. I ah be back." BH replied getting out, pulling the hoody over his head with the jewelry still wrapped in it.

"You got me fucked up. Henny got them! Where you go, I go." Vanessa stated.

After BH got the call from G-law, for whatever selfish reason. He figured he would leave by his self to probably end up dead or back in jail. Not at all. She reminded him he promised he wouldn't kill for money again. He wasn't killing for money. He told her how Fatts had 100k on him and 50k each on stacks, pezzy, and henny. He told her if he didn't get his man now, that there forever together was most likely another month or so.

"If a mafucka Tryna kill you Eujean, why you want me to stay here' t don't wanna live without you. I'm Comin or you not goin?" She stated with finality. He let her have the wheel.

Now he thought she would let him back into the streets at two in the morning with a dead man jewelry and brains wrapped in his hoody, alone! Try again motherfucker. She told him. "I'm not leaving this out here." BH said. cradling the jewelry and brains as if it was one of his babies.

"Yo fuckin head too damn big for you to be actin this stupid. Ain't no telling how many people we just killed – "

"Check spot news. "He said cutting off.

"- and you wanna bring evidence where us and our kids lay their head! Think. Eujean, please."

She left him outside. She had the key. He

Wasn't going anywhere in the Beemer. She took the guns and put them in the second fireproof safe. She was bringing damaging evidence in the house herself, but these were the only two guns BH had left. Their sole protection. Her adrenaline was still pumping. She hadn't shot a gun in years. While she shoot at the boys on the porch, she saw vivid in her mind now, BH step up and blew the back of that man's head out. It made her pussy drip sweet wet juices to see him bend down fluidly and carefully remove the jewelry from his neck. She was playing in her pussy while showering, thinking about the man of her dreams. The man in her life right now.

BH appeared behind her. wrapping his arms around her as she was climaxing. Rubbing brick (vanessa named it) in her juices.

"Who taught you how to throw (shoot) like that?", BH asked. standing behind her in the shower.

He was rubbing his dick on her pussy from The back. Vanessa arched her back for him and him Slipped inside her, she angled one of her legs Up on the edge of the tub, and bounced slowly on Him as he plucked her clit with his left hand, and her nipples with the right. Turning her head to face him, she offered her toque and he accepted it.

"OH, I'm cumin! Cum in me." She exclaimed and BH complied. She commanded every part of him. Mind body, and soul. Both knew it.

They finished showering together. Unable to keep their hands off each other. Into the bedroom with nothing except a towel cinched around them. BH was Getting hard walking with his dick between her thick cheeks.

"I want some more. "Vanessa begged in a voice so fuckin provocative it would be solely responsible for the way he was finna bone the fuck out her. Henny, asleep in their bed. She was pushing back on BH enticingly.

"Come on." BH turned her around with his left hand on her hip. He held his dick with the right, rubbing it on her wet wet from the back.

He stopped outside   their   bedroom,

directing her to the Top of the carpeted stairs like the pornstar he swore he is. He spread the dry towel over the stairs diagonally.

"Face down, ass up babe." He instructed her. Obediently she placed her hands on the top of the landing. Her feet planted six stairs from the top. She earned A+ for putting that ass up and out. Eye level with the prettiest pussy he'd ever seen, BH wasted no time putting his face in it. Making her scream his name as he cursed both holes equally.

"BH ... Un nun ... What. You ... Tryna. ... Do ... To ... Me ...", she moaned as she came hard all over his face.

Looking back at him, she saw her cream all over his lips like melted ice cream. She couldn't resist using Her tongue to help him clean his lips and chin. She felt him climb on top her a split second before he put his rock-hard dick inside her excited, twitching hot pussy. The impossible happened.

She came instantly.

"Un, un, I'm cumin!" She breathed out unbelievably.

"Stop lyin." BH gritted although he could feel the. Juices drenching him in evidence.

This mafucka just made me a minute woman. Vanessa thought as he went deep in her soaking wet Killa catcher.

He was touching the bottom effortlessly. He was pulling all the way out to tip, pushing back in slow and sensually.

But she felt Some type of way about him making her cum prematurely. She tightened her pussy muscles unexpectedly, trapping His dick for as long as her wet wet would allow.

Then Let go. She repeated this move a few more times. Fucking his head up.

"Fuck ... Schemer. Do that shit."

Yeah, yo turn nigga. Vanessa thought vindictively.

As she as she locked her vagina like a macaroni and cheese casserole and threw it back. He tried to grip her waist

And pound her out, but she kept her grip and wiggled Her thick hips from side to side like a playful red nosed Pit-bull and felt yet another nut building.

" Ahhh." BH growled losing the war to hold on for dear life. Exploding all In vanessa. She came right with him as he collapsed softly on top other ... BH its yours. She promised as she cherished his dick in her as it went soft.

"Infinitely." He asked out of breath.

"Infinitely." Vanessa confirmed.

* * * *

" Henny. This dress the one ain't it?" vanessa asked.

They were downtown in Neiman Marcus looking for her a birthday dress, a day before her twenty second birth right. The dress in question was a black v cut Christian Dior with gold paw prints.

" that's the one." henny cosigned. Admiring how the dress caressed Vanessa's slim, thick frame.

It didn't matter what she had on. Her big apple shaped booty with the slightly, bowed legs always popped in anything

She wore. Vanessa was a chocolate beauty. Inside and out. She made any outfit she threw on no matter if it was jeans and sneakers.

"I'm finna dress BH to the nines. She said to herself More so than henny, pausing.

She dazed off into a daydream. Her love for him was beyond real. And strong.

Something she felt with every part of her anatomy. "what you bout ta get for him? You are buying that dress?"

"Some boss shit to match a boss bitch. Yeah, I'm getting This. We need to go to Macys so I can find the kids some. We goin out to eat tomorrow. at twelve tonight im

Shakin my ass all on my man in some body club." Vanessa Danced happily as she peeked back at her voluptuous derrière in the mirror. She bit down sexily on her bottom lip thinking about BH with his face back there.

"I'm shakin my ass too hoe. broke bones and all." They Laughed as henny gave her seat a sexy little dance.

" y'all Went and fixed treasure name yesterday?"

"You know BH wasn't having that. Yep, she a Fulton now." Her and BH went downtown because BH wanted his daughter with his name.

She was a part of his legacy. He also opened up

Three trust funds. One each for jr., treasure, and eujeana.

Five thousand each, he promised to keep building

Them for as long as he lived. This way, when they turned eighteen, God forbid something was to happen to either of their parents, financially they will always be secure.

"a real man. Not a real nigga, bitch yo black ass blessed." Henny said. Finish with their shopping, they went back to vanessa hose to drop off nearly twelve thousand dollars' worth of gear.

"The other side keep taken big I's. fatts funeral tomorrow. I should go shake my ass at his casket."

They laughed at henny silliness as henny sat across her and BH bed.

"Show yo ass in their girl, them niggas gone act a fool."

Vanessa replied, setting the bags in the closet.

"They sayin he cheated his connect out a hundred bricks, El Chapo sent a hit team to get that ass." Vanessa laughed knowingly. "I'm for real bitch!" Henny said seriously, thinking vanessa was laughing at her

And not with her. henny felt her source was platinum.

Wordlessly, vanessa went to the safe BH kept his guns in, opened it and removed the double Zip lock bag that held the jewelry big head removed from fatts neck.

She didn't know where or how but he had gotten The man's blood and brain tissue off the chains and Charms, coming out the closet, she sat the jewelry on the bed next to henny who was on snap chat, fatts was the reason her best friend was almost killed and hopping around with broken bones leveled in a cast.

" what's that?" henny asked, recording a snap. Not paying

Attention that she had half a million dollars sitting next to her.

"Get That Phone Out yo Face bitch and pay attention. That's why you still a sophomore in this shit now."

Vanessa said playfully.

"Hoe, you fucked up my snap." Henny smacked her lips, looking down beside her.

The biggest charm was a big diamond encrusted L with the word station behind it she looked at Vanessa with her mouth open wide with surprise . Didn't take a rocket scientist to know who the jewelry belonged to or how vanessa got it .

"Close yo math before a dick fly in it." Vanessa fell across the bed laughing hard at the look on henny face was so funny.

She was in her phone and no longer paying any Attention to henny who was still in shock. Her source Wasn't shit. Vanessa was texting BH to see when she could get some head and dick.

While vanessa was in her phone, ass in the air Practicing how she would do BH. henny had put the c" station" chain around her neck, and was recording a snap mugged up. Henny sent that snap, she now wanted vanessa to go in one with her .

"bitch get the guns and do a snap with me."
"hell Naw bitch. I showed you that so you know that hit team was for you . Not snap chat. Vanessa snapped knowing better.

"Matter fact. Let me put this shit up. "she got The jewelry and put it back inside the safe.

Somewhere on the other side.....

The G big dip sat watching henny snap chat from His dead sons cell phone. He couldn't believe she Was on there with fatts j' on. If she had access To jewelry his killers took. that mean folks nem across

The bully (boulevard) had something to do with stone getting changed (killed)

Now that he thought on it, lil Greg (G- law) was wrap tight with them dudes tough when they was babies.

Just so happen, stone nem dropping like flies. when one Of our own posed to be securing the nation. G dip thought. Ima demo(demonstrate) with g-law myself. He concluded snatching up his 44. Magnum.

CHAPTER FOURTEEN

"Schemer, get the car while I get the kids." BH passed. Her the valet ticket for the car. They were leaving a five star soul food restaurant called. Aunt Ree's downtown. vanessa and treasure both were dressed in Burberry dresses while BH and jr. ., together had on Burberry Polo out fits. henny, stacks, yazzy, pezzy, lucky and her guy. t-nator and His wife. g-law and toya were present out front of aunt Ree's when The valet attendant arrived with the 2017 smoke gray land rover range rover v8 super charged on 22 inch forgiatos, big red bow tie on the hood instead of the X6 they came in.

"Happy birthday schemer." BH said enchanted.

vanessa turned, and found him on bended knee with a small box of ice presented to her. vanessa smiled hard before dropping her head to hide the tears escaping her eyes.

"Girl lift yo head and let that man see your joy." Lucky encouraged while her and several others recorded the moment For Facebook, Instagram, snapchat and a few other social media Outlets. vanessa did as her big sister said and stepper in front of BH.

"Blessin after blessin I done caught. Including the blessing Of catchin your heart. It's true. I know its ah god and that together Forever it's our hearts, destined to never be apart. In the light or deep in darkness, infinitely my schemer, I'll cherish your spark. 1st in anything you my everything. Marry me vanessa? "

With hands wet from swiping away tears, vanessa reached out to bring BH to his feet.

"You for real?" Vanessa asked softly through a water fall of blinding tears. Body pressed into his.

"Fasho." BH confirmed. "Marry me schemer?"

"Fa sho." She echoed.

BH placed the three-carat princess cut vvs solitary

Diamond set in white gold ring on her left
hand. Half the diners in 'Aunt Rees' stepped out
to see what was going on.

All applauded the young couple.

The range rover ran him close to eighty
thousand. The princess but diamond, another
seventy-five. T-nator covered both in exchange
for the Chicago bulls' charm and chain.

BH pocketed twenty-five the sand in cash
and still Held two chains and charms. The hit on
Fatts put him in the big league instantaneously.
A prime example on how

Something so personal turns out to be great
for business.

Mothers were called. First Vanessa's. Then
big Heads. All ended up at Vanessa's mothers
house with their mothers and families overly
excited.

Vanessa's father Lived out of town with his
wife, but wished vanessa and BH a
congratulations via video chat on Facebook.

Her birthday dinner easily transformed into
an engagement party. Her and BH were
inseparable. No one existed outside of their love

bubble. She snuggled up under him on her mother's couch up her love.

"For me BH …. the best birthday ever." Vanessa said in a low tone, dreamily admiring her three-carat engagement ring.

"On big homie, I'm given you nothing but the best." BH replied. Admiring her.

Wrapped up comfortably up under each other, they drank the night away with loved ones and vibe, oblivious to the

Recent traumas endured if only for the moment. Everybody got so intoxicated enjoying themselves, majority who was there ultimately stayed the night.

Morning came with Vanessa waking BH with kisses all over his face.

"Big head. Get up so we can go home and fuck."

" I heard that lil girl." Vanessa's mom dukes said coming down the stairs.

I'm series ma. I didn't even get no birthday sex. Vanessa pated.

"Yoo." BH yawned. "I'm up, I'm up."

"Y'all can leave the kids here." Mrs. Daniels offered, without a second thought, BH went in his pocket and peeled her mother five crispy hundreds.

Thank you, son." She said gratefully.

"No problem. Let me throw some water on my face and we

Can go schemer." BH said, excusing his self. While he was taking a piss, his phone rang. "Yoo?" He answered seeing it was kc.

"Congrats. You all over the book and Instagram on bended Knee like you me." Kc laughed good natured.

"Good looking." BH replied.

"You still on top of the soft?", he inquired. Referring to the cocaine.

"Yeah, I'm doin a lil some."

"I got a play for two blocks." He threw out there, but big head couldn't figure out why he didn't cut into nick when that's who they all went through.

"I got a block left I done broke down. Why you ain't get up with nick?" It domed (came to mind) on him a split second before kc said anything.

"80 down the middle. If you leave em there." He promised schemer he wouldn't kill for money again. But damn, the temptations was his favorite movie.

"When you wanna make it happen?"

"Soon as you come out side, I'm on the block now."

"Aiight. Give me a few hours. Ima pop at bout one."

"Sayless, Ima line it up. Love."

"Love." BH finished up in the bathroom.

"Who was that?" schemer questioned as he came cut into the hallway.

"Ah money move. You ready?" he loved how attentive vanessa is. she matched his fly. aggressiveness, freakiness, and intelligence amongst other things.

The love of his life was beyond beautiful and
The definition of a bad bitch. A real woman.
And a great mother. *I wouldn't trade this lady
in for nothing in the universe.* he thought
lovingly.

"Ah money move? You Comin home with
me right?"

Her question was rhetorical. he ensnared
her waist and let her taste the mint tooth paste
he rinsed his mouth out with.

"Ugg! Mama got old people toothpaste."

"lil girl ain't nothing old in this house.
Everything is fine like wine."

Mrs. Daniels capped from the kitchen." You
are so young I bet you not given it up like this."

She hit a full split in the middle of the kitchen
With only her house coat and some pajamas on.
BH eyes were Open so wide, vanessa and Mrs.
Daniels both folded with laughter. Mrs. Daniels
was a little on the heavy side, so it most
definitely caught him by surprise.

"Really! In the kitchen ma?!" vanessa laughed while trying to drink orange juice.

"Since all my kids grown. Me and my husband enjoy ourselves all over this house."

"Ma!" Vanessa spat her orange juice out embarrassed. BH stood

Mouth wide open now also. Stuck. Her og fell out laughing.

"Bighead close yo mouth and come on. Ma you too old to be that nasty."

"Yo og still got it." BH said half-jokingly as they walked out the front door.

"You wanna stay here with her?" BH turned around to go back in the house and vanessa playfully snatched A handful of his dreads.

"Ahh crazy ass girl." he laughed

"Don't fuckin play with me."

They got in the range rover and took off with Vanessa man handling the super charged us like a true Vet. BH called pezzy who was at least able to drive

Now that he was healing properly. He prep pezzy to come coop him in a few hours. BH knew his boy was flat on his back broke. The loud has lane before them slugs lamed hill out.

The ten thousand he would hit dizzy with to have The wheel would give him a little traction to get Right on his feet. As soon as he got rid of the rest Of the jewelry, the plan was to break bread and situate Pezzy with another thirty to forty thousand. Schemer was Playing this new song by king Deazal featuring g -Herbo called "pull up"

His mind wasn't really on the money move. During Those six years under lock, his mentor big herc From no love city told him, the greatest wealth a Black man can have been a wife and his own family.

He looked over at vanessa and knew that he wanted to be the one for her, They would slide together, get high together.

enjoy Life together and no doubt overcome any struggle

Together.
RAYVON PARKER   176

The most important was for them to have the Pleasure to grow old and float off into eternity together.

BH couldn't believe his thoughts was set on growing old, but with her was where he wanted to be infinitely.

Driving up to the house, they saw the x6 parked in Front the garage. Vanessa reversed the range in next to his Beemer. She jumped out the truck like her Pants was on fire and he followed her inside the house.

BH received a text message from ro roast vanessa stripped her clothes and headed for the shower with her come fuck me face.

Ro ro: Wassup with the u(jewelry) you was talkin about??

BH: I'ma htl (hit the line) later.

ro ro: whatever * kissy face emoji

Sitting his phone down, he quickly undressed and

Went in the master bathroom with vanessa who was standing back from the water with soap suds all over her.

Stepping inside the tub, he reached over and removed the was Cloth from her hands. BH proceeded to wash her chest, neck, Stomach, and pussy, in that order positioning her to face Him, he washed her back. Sides. And between her cheeks before kneeling to one knee and washing her legs each foot thoroughly.

"Thank you." Vanessa said appraisingly. This was another has for her. No man' ever catered to her so sensually and here. This known killer is, being the ultimate gentleman.

Blew her mind. BH never ceased to amaze her. Standing,

BH detached the universal shower head and rinsed her off. Back down on one knee, he directed her to place her left foot on the edge of the tub. He adjusted the Pressure of the water and let the stream pestle over her Swollen pearl. Licking it while never moving the trajectory of the water, tongue and water tag teamed her clit until it was ready to explode its release.

"Uhm, shit." She moaned dizzily, feeling two of his fingers enter her box.

BH licked, kissed, sucked, and fingered the pussy until he tasted her cum all over his lips. Vanessa fell weight less Into his arms as he stood his right hand palming her left Cheek, he tapped her right leg with his lefthand gesturing with his head for her to jump up in his arms.

Vanessa, trusting him, hopped up and he caught her. BH placed her back to the shower wall as the water Attempted to divide them. She reached down and put Him inside her with a such of gratification while Their tongues danced. Legs strong, he sat on the edge of the tub and let her bounce in his lap, she couldn't resist biting his neck for a distraction. Okay hurt so good.

At some point, in between the shifting of positions, they exited the tub and BH penetrated her from behind. On pure instinct their eyes locked in the mirror. Vanessa reached back and spread her thick ass chocolate cheeks and he lost the war.

"You knew that move was gone make me bust." he stated after pumping the last of his seed deeply into her. It better. She capped back, turning her head to the side for a kiss.

****
****

Nick fronted BH two blocks (bricks) of coke with no Problem. BH didn't confide in him that he was fixing To use them as bait to wrap a mafucka up.

All nick Needed to know is that it was a play BH had in effect for some major money. He can't want his sixty even back.

It was apparent he wanted to see big head Come Into his own. He knocked six points off each block. BH could've made a nice profit without leaving them stretched, but what the fuck?

Pezzy didn't fall through for whatever reason so BH linked up with one of the guys named milli. Folks Wasn't a killer but was at least reliable behind the wheel and would keep his mouth shut. BH would give him five bands and still hit pezzy with five though he wasn't on point.

Him and mile camper out on the dead end across Halsted on the 9 (59th). Kc had it set for a couple p niggas from Rockford, Illinois to pull up and cop.

BH and milli were inside this hype (crackhead) name Jan crib. If it was left up to him, BH wanted to Knock dude nem shit back in Jan spot and leave ire There. Jan cried and the whole nine yards, begging BH not to kill nobody in her house.

Kc dead that plan of action although it Was empty and seemed abandoned, only things saving face is the flat screen, couch and PlayStation y in the Living room for kc workers when they jammed out her spot. If God willed it, BH killed it. Inside or out didn't matter to him. The time had arrived.

BH was sitting on the couch kicking ass with Bruce lee on ps4 when kc called to inform him Dude nem would be there in a few minutes. Milli drove a white alaro. BH told him to go lay back in it and be ready to exit stage left.

Pezzy would choose to call right then and there To ask where they were.

"in motion." BH responded to his inquire.

"Big head wait on me bitch!"

" I'm on one right now. Ima hit yo line when it's done. I got you."

" Where you at bitch?"

"I got you Brody." BH disconnected the call seeing kc number light up the screen.

U-G Was outside. BH sent Jan out to Open the door while he remained seated with a. 357 Sig Sauer on his lap, playing the crane this big six Foot five-inch tall bald mafucka with a full Beard and his face permanently twisted, walked in the spot behind Jan.

He had a short squirrel looking nigga with him. Both wore louis Vuitton man bags over their shoulders and laying over their chest that matched the Louie v head to toe gear they had on.

"What's up g." the bald head giant said, reaching hand out to BH. Any mafucka taller than hats five feet Seven inches was a giant in his eyes.

"What's the word, you u-G?"

"Yeah folks. I'm ugly, get ugly-U-G. you feel me?" he grabbed BH hand and they locked pitch forks.

Kc was a global gangster. It didn't surprise BH That he was in tune with some official GD's out Rockford, Illinois. Willing to back door (snake) them, nonetheless.

After all, he is the king cobra. BH could tell U-G. Was like that (a killer). It wasn't just in his Mug. His energy radiated it.

He would close these accounts accordingly and fast knowing he couldn't underestimate him.

"Fa sho. I'm BH my nigga. Let me grab these blocks. BH made Jan get the coke, her small wood table, and the scale kc had there.

U-g pulled his own scale out of his Louie bag Along with four bundles of money. The lil nigga followed Suit and BH saw the handle of something chunky on Standby. U-G cut into both the blocks in different spots. snorting a small line from each one. the nigga had to sit down and stand back up six times.

"True fish scale indeed." U-G Said this with genuine respect.

"A, y'all know this dude y'all way name goony c?"

"We don't fuck wet dude. he from the west side. Albert And Andrews."

"Where anybody would die." BH rapped automatically repeating what his man's goony c told him when they were cellies. He was a solid vice lord that got 75 years for some fluky shit that wasn't on him. I was locked up with him." BH offered.

"yeah! We into its wit them." The squirrel looking nigga added and it sealed his fate. BH had mad love for goony c. U-G was geeked

"Din din give that money." he said. Teeth chattering.

Din din passed the four bundles of money from

His Louie man bag over. BH and van counted through All eight bundles like professional bank tellers. Eighty thousand.

"y'all str8." BH placed the eighty thou in his small Gucci backpack and told Jan that he would walk them out.

Din Din put the two blocks of coke in his Louie bag while u-g put the scale back into his.

The three of them stepped out the house together.

" BH, you got a lighter?" u-g turned around with a Newport cigarette in his mouth. Big head shot

Him once between the eyes. His signature.

Boom!

Boom! Boom boom!

The next three went in the back of din din head. Parting his shit like the scene in terminator

When he split the liquid metal mafucka in half With the pump at the end. BH yanked the

Louie

Vuitton man bag up off din din and walked
Calmly up the dead end where milli was
parked. Only the people from this block
knew that Wasn't a dead end and that it
opened Back up to Halsted Street, milli was
charged As BH got in the passenger seat. He
mashed the gas. scratching off, turning hard
through the Cut speeding. The cut that
opened back up to Halsted was wide open.
If twelve was on Halsted, the move would
have been fronted.

This made him miss henny having the wheel.

" Chill out and slow down." BH snapped,
adrenaline pumping.

" On big homie! You fucked them up in lire
two seconds!!"

" Drive regular to the block milli." he had
eighty thousand, two bricks of coke and a pole
with two bodies on it in his possession. *If we get
pulled over, I'm doing this nigga.*

BH thought wickedly putting his seat belt
On. Milli made it on the block and be called
kc. Not two minutes later, kc slithered out
the

Passenger seat of a black ss trail blazer with a Pull over hoody on. He approached the driver side. BH thought he was gesturing for milli to let the Window down.

Bloaw!

A shot rang out and mille brain tissue Smacked him flush in the face. Blinding him. Frantically Trying to get his homie brains and blood out his eyes, he threw his left arm up while searching for the passenger door handle with his other hand. Boom! Bloaw ... Boom boom boom!

BH felt slug after slug slam into Him as he fall out milli car. Eyes now open more From pain and shock, then clear of brain matter, he Saw kc running around the front of the car, probably To deliver the coup de grace to his head. The Sig was sitting on the passenger seat having been In its usual spot under his right leg. Out of Reach. He dug inside the. Louis Vuitton man bag And wrapped his hand around a thick revolver, dragging it free, he snooze the fat trigger with no energy to Aim.

Ka- boom!

CHAPTER FIFTEEN...VANESSA

Vanessa flinched out of her pleasure induced sleep knowing something was terribly wrong. Throwing the silk sheets from her curvaceous body, she got up from the California king sized bed and called out for BH.

"Eujean?!" She called out for him a few more times moving naked throughout their home. She was near hysterical and unbearably cold. Discombobulated, she couldn't grasp why.

Snatching up her phone, she saw that it was dead. She Plugged it into its charger before going and getting in the shower. Even the piping hot shower water wouldn't warm her nor calm her nerves.

Her iPhone automatically powered itself when it obtained a significant amount of battery. It started To ring incessantly ". She rushed from the shower with soap covering all over her chocolate body. Stomach hurting so bad she was folded over at the waist when she answered.

"Yeah, ma? "She groaned.

"Vanessa where are you?" Her mother was asking. She was in so much pain, she couldn't respond. Her head and heart was now aching in tandem with her stomach.

"They just killed them boys."

Her mother yelled the last part into the Phone, more pain racked Vanessa's book, making her drop her phone. Now she understood the pain though she rested to acknowledge what was being told to her.

" I'm on my way out there to you vanessa." her mother

Disconnected the call. Vanessa's phone was blowing up

Back-to-back with calls from what seemed everyone her and but knew. She didn't want to hear it again from Anyone that wasn't there. God heard her. Evidently. BH telling pezzy To come get him on their ride home had her hyperventilating when pezzy Name and number filled her screen. Beyond terrified, she answered. All she Could do is hold the phone and bawl like a baby.

''Sus stop all that crying and get up we down here at northwestern. You know my nigga ah soldier.

"pezzy what happen ?!', vanessa blinked back the tears. She was literally dying from a crippled heart.

"Big head got shot. Get down here and let everybody else think he gone.''

''Alright.'' Was all she responded with. She got up, washed boogers

The snot from her face. she put on a Nike track Suit, air max, secured her gun and keys and was out the door. Her mother called, worried, vanessa let her know to Keep the kids.

She was okay. Racing downtown, she didn't Answer her phone for anyone. When she got to northwestern hospital, she called pezzy. He sent the boy pistol to come down and get her.

'He got hit twice. Once in the arm, once in the side, he good tho sus.

"What happen!? Why everybody sayin he dead?!" vanessa spat.

Ready to kill the city behind bringing harm to the love of her life. never mind being sad or hurt. Though pistol and pezzy kept reiterating that he was str8, she needed to see him and be the judge of that.

"Where he at?"

"The ICU."

When they entered the intensive care unit, BH Was sitting up in the hospital bed looking high as Giraffe pussy. Rushing over to him, she threw herself in His arms. She didn't care that he was hunt now that she saw he was alive. It was her that needed to feel Him in order to heal her. She broke down. exposing

The child she was deep inside.

Loosening Her hold on him, she caught her breath enough to ask questions.

" Big head what's goin on?!"

" This hoe ass nigga killed milli." BH replied hoarsely.

She knew Enough not to question it any further right then and there.

BH told them to get the doctor. He was leaving already knowin 12 would be there soon. Hospitals had an obligation to report all gunshot victims upon admission.

BH told her how his blood was probably all in milli car and on the ground outside of it where he Fell. Milli baby mama already Told the 12-bighead called milli and that they were together. Blood was all over the ground. The hood of the car. And inside. Even Tina, milli baby mama believed BH was dead. It was all over Facebook and Instagram.

They We're looking at pictures of the bloody scene on vanessa on social media

Phone, it was plastered. With no regard for the families. Vanessa helped him into the new clothes pistol new ran

And not for him prior to her arrival. As they were Leaving, the icu area where his bed was located, a Doctor pointed them out to a group of police officers who speedily approached.

"Mr. Fulton! I'm detective stanic. We need to speak with you before you leave.

BH winced as if he was in great pain. His left Arm was in a cast and his left side and back was bandaged from where the bullet entered and exited.

" Ion know who shot me. Come on schemer."

" It's a bit more complicated than that, we believe. A Friend of yours; kwamane Dixon, was shot and killed around 1:30 to 2:30 pm. About the time you arrived here with gunshot wounds. We found blood and two firearms on the Scene. believed to have been used in the murder and Shooting of not only you and your friend, but two D.O.A(dead on arrival)

Victim's a few blocks over. The community where these Murders occurred seem to believe you've been killed as Well. That's most interesting to us care to explain. "

"am I being charged with anything? " BH asked, and vanessa heart nearly stopped.

"Currently, no. Maybe you will clear some things for us? There was blood on the front of Mr. Dixon's car. Some found on the ground next to a firearm . Is this your blood or does this blood and gun belong to the man who shot You and killed Mr. Dixon?"

"I don't know who shot me. Somebody ambushed the car as I was gettin in and open fire. I covered my face and that's the last I remember officer."

"We're detectives. How long were you and Mr. Dixon inside the Car together before someone opened fire on the two of You?"

"Officer I'm In a lot of pain and my family is concerned about my well-being. Do you have a card so I can get back to you?"

" Sure." The black detective wearing a bow tie responded. passing BH a card.

"make sure you contact us within twenty-four hours."

"Aiight. Come on vanessa." BH and vanessa departed the hospital to find pezzy and pistol amongst several guys waiting near her range rover.

"My nigga! you was right on time." BH said to pezzy genuinely grateful.

"Better late than never." Pezzy replied and they hugged tightly.

"Grab them bags. "BH told him.

Vanessa was helping him sit in the range's passenger Seat. Pezzy sent one of the dudes with him over to his jeep. The guy came back with a louis Vuitton man bag and a Small Gucci backpack.

"Here." BH passed pezzy two bricks of money. He reached in the other bag and gave him a large square of cocaine

Vanessa assumed was a whole brick.

"Ion think nick or t-nator had they hand in this pot. Right now, ion give no fuck, that's all you tho. Get back with me if yo gone re-up. That's twenty too. "

" Forever my brother -", pezzy started.

"-my brother, my love." BH completed Making his lady smile.

" Big head bitch." Pezzy smiled also and they embraced again hard.

Pezzy nem watched BH and vanessa leave the parking area before they left. Her mother face timed her as she is getting on the expressway.

" Wassup ma." vanessa answered holding the phone down by the gear shift so as not to get curbed by 12.

Her mother had a stricken look on her face. You could tell she was devastated behind the news with big head. That he had been killed.

"What you gone tell them babies' schemer?"

"Ma, you did not just call me schemer?" Vanessa laughed.

"Yes, I did. It made you laugh, didn't it? That young man Kept a smile on to face and I really love him for Stepping up with my grand babies." her mother cried openly expressing these sentiments.

Vanessa glanced over at big head with tears of her own in her eyes.

''I know right.'' Vanessa cosigned and those tears escaped her eyes. Bh reached over with his right hand and wiped her tears away.

Vanessa who in the hell is that puttin they dirty ass Hands in yo face. Mrs. Daniels went from grieving to Hot in a flash thinking her daughter was callous enough At this moment To be with another man . When BH turned the Phone camera on him, she screamed and dropped the phone. Thank you, lord Jesus! Thank you, Jesus. She said this excitedly maybe ten times.

"Ma." Vanessa said a few times to Calm her down .

"Ma don't say nothing. They killed his friend land he got shot two times."

" No. I won't. That's stills bad. Big head I love you son. Y'all call me when y'all make it home." She hung up thanking Jesus.

Vanessa sped home and helped BH inside Though he was alright. One bullet cracked the bone

In his forearm and the bullet in his side came out his back without damaging anything. He assured vanessa the shit hurt, but he was good. "Do you not know who shot you?" she asked After running him a hot bath and pouring a whole Bottle of green rubbing alcohol in it.

"Yeah. the hoe ass nigga kc tried to snake me For 80 bands and two blocks." BH shook his head.

Kc raised him and was one of the first people to show him how to kill. Vanessa knew exactly who King cobra was, that he was rich and a killer.

What she couldn't understand is why snake BH ?

"So, what now? I mean, I'm ready for whatever. I ah this and that ah mafucka for you. Better know it." She pledged while bathing him.

"Fa sho. I hit em somewhere in the chest with something chunky. Shit, he might be dead somewhere. He better be."

"Are we cool stayin here?"She asked looking him in his eyes.

"Naw, not really. Not right now at least. We gone tuck until I find out what's what. I got ah couple things to situate and we ah be a hunnid."

Her heart hurt every time she let him leave their house. headed back into a field of treachery, hate and greed amongst other things. the pain she woke up to this evening confirmed That they are attached mind, body , and soul. She Rather die than live alone to endure a cutting pain so deep. This man is my everything and I am his. Vanessa mused emotionally.

"Schemer, you my everything first in anything." He stated and

   She flinched

She shouldn't have been surprised though that has sentiments reflected her musings.

"You are mine. last to none." She whispered.

   "I love your schemer."

   "I love you more."

      "I love you infinitely."

   "And I love you more then all that." Vanessa promised.

Somewhere on the other side ....

G-law was blessed with a calm, cool, collected mind. Which was almost never conflicted. It wasn't that He was incapable of showing emotion, he just naturally didn't.

It was all over the other side about his brother Big head being killed earlier in the day. The moes were out Poppin bottles and shaking ass harder than the females, they were so happy. Glaw was present and all smiles. When anything of significance went down involving your family and you wasn't hip to the facts true and or false, you didn't sincerely care for that person, or you simply wasn't family. Before BH made it to northwestern hospital, pezzy

Was on the phone with g-law. Giving him a b low by blow as BH gave it to him. G-law was immediately checking every hospital in the city to see if anyone with

Wound to the chest had been brought in. Best believe g-law would have pulled the plug or threw additional slugs on kc with no hesitation. Pezzy told g-law that him and BH had a money move lined up with king cobra but yazzy was running around the house with his iPhone. She didn't want pezzy on no hot shit when he could hardly stand on his own two feet for more than a few minutes. Pezzy was beyond grateful for yazzy playing with his phone. It would be him dead instead of milli.

Pezzy ate a lil pussy and finessed his phone from yazzy. By then BH was with Kwa milli. After BH wouldn't tell him where they were, pezzy figured he would link up With kc and big head on the block. Pezzy saw the ss trail blazer fly past him but didn't think nothing of it. He was banging Chicago artist king Deazal music so loud he couldn't say if he heard any shots fared.

When he drove down the block, he saw milli And big head. BH had crawled over toward aunt may Porch and passed out. Him and one of the family hypes on the block named John Jr. got BH inside his jeep.

He dialed g-law as john Jr, slapped big head Into consciousness. G-law was one of the main

People helping to spread the rumor that BH was a goner.

"G - law!" He turned around to see his first cousin.

"Poochy. "he smiled sincerely.

"Wassup stone." He erected the pyramid with him using The index fingers before slapping the five.

"The g dip looking for you suh. "

" On stone I been hearing that. What's the demonstration. " g-law was asking for what.

"Some pipes, I heard. "Poochy raised his eyebrows with that. The g dip owned three or four rigs and owned his own trucking company.

"I'm out here all night. He should have my number."

"Want me to give it to em? "if Poochy gave G-dip a

Number on -law, both knew nothing but a bullet to the head would answer.

"Naw. He well if he do or don't got it." G-law didn't even finish the Budweiser he was sippin.

When his cousin got lost in the crowd, he went to his car and switched his registered 40. Smith and Wesson for the throw away . 40 he kept in the slot. It was do or die. He had a lot more years to live out here in the windy city.

"Can I Get a square?" G-Law looked over to see

Shay shay posing like a pretty ass model. Everybody knew G-law didn't smoke. Cigarettes and or weed. he flashed his shark like smile nonetheless.

"Ion smoke. I ah but you a pack though. "She walked around to the passenger side and got in his car. Crazy as this was, no one noticed.

CHAPTER SIXTEEN

A smooth week since big head was Shot and the homie milli killed for reasons still BH was ghost.

Unknown to everyone, the windy city was going To continue being wined regardless of the season what when where and why, BH, vanessa, and their children, Eujeana included, were Up in Orlando, Florida at the Disney world resort.

The day following big head getting shot, he did The opposite of what the police on television warned you not to do when you were a person of interest in A crime. He tasked vanessa with setting it in motion for them to exit stage left and take a vacation from The madness of the life in Chicago right now. Things Moving too fast back home. The only way to slow It all down, was to change the scenario not for self his whole family.

The kids were over enjoying themselves. Still with

A cast on his arm and a hole in his side and back, Big head was heavily involved in all the activities His lady planned for them as a family. He was happy to be alive and showing it.

The only thing that bothered him at this moment In time; is, back in Chicago, now he was wanted for Questioning in the double murder of the two out Of town niggas from Rockford. Kc turned up at 17 hospitals out in Gary, Indiana, his dead body was Dropped off later that day with a gunshot To the chest. From a . 410 revolver. Powerful.

That was good news to BH. kc blood would be Kc's blood would be identified as the doner to the blood on the hood Of milli car, the. 357 sig Sauer had already been Linked to the double murder the gun kc dropped Was also confirmed as the weapon that killed Milli and used in the shooting of BH. Bumps rapped it best smile even when you down / never let em see you sweat.

Vanessa knew none of this. Right now, with how happy her and the kids are, he isn't liable to tell her. He just wouldn't spoil their vacation.

Nick and t-nator was the source supplying The information, and updates via the high price

Team of lawyers they hired to figure out what was Going on. T-nator and pezzy was communicating. BH Changed his number to stop his phone from ringing, d select few had it back in the city of no lung. Pezzy, g-law, and his mother, His brother had been so low that he was Especially with the move the sucker to pulled on him. When BH expressed to his mother how he felt, she responded with.

"Eujean, DeShawn Alright."

"you talked to em?! " he asked hopefully. "nope. Yet I trust in God. I know when something is wrong wit one of mine."

Big head left it at that. Now he was standing Now he was standing Here under the hot Florida sun at Disney world recording his daughter sit upon a dolphin while he held

Eujeana, she bounced up and down in his one good arm. In excitement for her turn.

"You next gee gee." BH promised her.

"Take jr. to pee big head. " vanessa said from next to him. she was recording treasure on her phone too and didn't want to miss anything, she had the brightest smile he'd seen on her face thus far.

"Gotta pee big man?" He asked jr. while passing eujeana to vanessa.

"Um huh." He responded Tryna finish off the cotton candy he was punishing. "Aiight, come on." BH needed to piss also now that he thought about it.

Him and jr. pimped through the resort with ralph Lauren cargo outfits and God blue clogs on.

They both went and relieved their bladders. When Jr. and BH returned from the restroom, he saw the dolphin handler now had a giggling Eujeana on the back of the dolphin. Vanessa had Ameerah on face time with her phone in Eujeana face. He could hear Ameerah talking to their daughter.

"Look at gee gee! Look at gee gee!" Ameerah was chanting and giggling as much as eujeana. BH took his phone back out and started to record.

"Where was the dolphin rides when we was lil girls. "Vanessa pouted.

"Okay!" Ameerah agreed.

It was all love to see both mothers of his babies with enough maturity alongside the self-respect they possessed to co -parent. BH let his

Inner child run wild the way him and jr. ran around the batman theme park, getting on every Ride. Dressing in a costume. And wanting to buy toys as much as jr. left and right. Everything there was to do over the seven days they'd been at Disney world. They did it.

All five of them were loaded with an abundance of items, toys, and souvenirs. So many that it would cost A couple thousand to ship all their stuff back to the city.

BH Splurged 10k or better with a feeling of peace, ready to blow a few more. Neither him nor vanessa were counting. This was truly the way to vacation.

The smiles that graced his family's-tired faces were more healing than the medication and creams. He barely noticed his wounds. Riding back to the hotel that night, an idea came to him.

" Schemer." he called over to her.

They were traveling in a chauffeured

Cadillac escalade. She was sitting next to him. The babies were all sleep on the back row across front them.

"Huh?", she responded, exhausted.

"What island you wanna get married on?" He asked. As they have conversed deeply over the cast Couple months, getting to know each other more intimately, He learned not only had she already been to several Islands, but in fact attended a cousins wedding down in the Virgin Islands and enjoyed herself immensely.

"We can get married right now. Right here in the back Of this truck if we together past all that infinitely shit." She related this to him serious and Straight faced. It warmed him inside out. Simplicity at its finest hour in his mind and heart.

"You sound like you know something I don't. What's more than infinitely schemer."

"How long me and you gone be together mafucka", she replied, and they both laughed.

The bell hop ran to retrieve a cart for the many purchases stuffed behind the truck when they arrived back at the hotel. The two of them were

So tired, vanessa fell asleep with big head dick in her hands. He with a handful of her thick Back side in his. As much as they wanted to fuck the night away, sleep conquered them. *

"Uhm." Vanessa moaned as she hijacked the dick of a sleeping BH. Initially she rode him slow and methodically, to get him hard as steel and as moist with her sweet milky creamy as an iced donut Stick, when she started to speed up and grind into his pelvic for more friction on her clit, he woke up.

"Damn." He exclaimed sleepily.

Palming her thick hips with his good hand, he motivated her to do her shit. Vanessa was really into it after BH kept the words of encouragement coming. He swore to her having the best pussy. The prettiest pussy. Lying flat with her breast on his bare chest, vanessa bit on his bottom lip as she bounced On him with sloppy wet sounds.

"Mommy." One of their kids called from the other side of their bedroom door.

Vanessa tightened her pussy. Pressed her chest to his and bounced even faster. Harder. Wetter. Driven towards her organism. BH was doing all the moaning her pussy was so extraordinarily good.

Vanessa put her lips folly over his, sucking on his tongue quietly him and they came hard. Together. As was usual between them by then. "Ma!" Treasure called. Vanessa leapt off him, snatching up her robe.

BH pulled the thousand count threaded comforter Over him while she opened the door for all three of the kids. His little soldiers wasted no time bum rushing their way past schemer.

"Daddy we hungry." This was Jr. . He'd been Calling BH daddy the entire time they were Down in Florida. It came so natural. So BH the Accepted honor, especially since Jr. biological Father was missing in action.

"Aiight big man. Tell me what you wanna eat a and Ima get it right now." BH said this leaning over to grab the hotel room phone. The presidential suite they occupied came with a kitchen Dining room And two bedrooms. Room service was still a perk and on point .

"I want blue berry waffles and cheese eggs. " jr. said.

"Me too." Treasure said, she was talking more.

"Me too!" Eujeana repeated behind her big sister. This was believed to be the encouragement in Building treasure's vocabulary. She was leading Her little sister . BH ordered blue berry Cheese eggs , turkey bacon, grapes and Orange juice for him and the kids. Vanessa got a steak omelet, pork bacon, sliced Banana and apple juice. The food was there in under thirty minutes flat.

The meal got Punished at the dinning room table as a family. Everyone was fed properly, the kids were next washed and dressed. After BH and vanessa took a power shower together with no sex, they all went shopping.

BH bought his beautiful black queen a all white form fitting Givenchy dress , she opted out for some pink Christian Louboutin heels. He got himself a matching all white Givenchy linen suit and loafers. The kids each were laced in dolce and Gabbana out fits. They left red where they stepped in the red bottom sneakers for children, BH had them all taken over to Miami-Dade courthouse where him and vanessa got married with only their kids there to witness it. "Whenever you ready my lady, we can do it real big." he said this referring to going all out on a real traditional wedding.

"This big enough. I'm Mrs. Eujean fulton. That's big enough. Thank you baby." she stated emotionally kissing his lips .

"Naw, thank you g. "he countered. It was official .. Mr., and Mrs. Fulton. VANESSA called her mother to tell her they went ahead and got married in Miami.

" Vanessa, I would be mad as hell if life wasn't so short for our young black men. I felt the loss personally when it was said my son-in-law was gone. Congratulations baby. "

"Thank you, ma." Vanessa teared up.

Her mother wasn't sad telling then the girl Shay Shay from the other side got killed a couple days Ago. It was reported on the news that she was shot More than ten times, crazy their plane was scheduled to. Land in Chicago late that night. Mrs. Daniels wanted Them to be careful.

"We can get a house down here if you want to."BH Offered.

"Tell ah bitch anything why don't you." Vanessa replied, like he was playing.

"Give me a month. Start looking for some now and I promise its yours. On big homie." He merched it.

Back in Chicago on the other side ....

Three five-star generals for the black p stones were

On the "one demonstrating (meeting). G red. G Tiwan . And the Was normal for them to step out and draw

With one another collectively to sort out what needed tube done for the other side. The three were out in the open on the one (51st). A couple blocks down from where lil dir. was brutally by a female.

" Say Tiwan. You remember the two short cousins' sherry and Joyce Fulton?"

" The twin cousins!" He laughed. Sherry and Joyce Fulton were first cousins but could pass for twin sisters easily.

" that's them Moe!" dip said excitedly as if he saw them vividly In his mind's eye.

" Yeah, sherry married the p (prince). "

" What about em Suh." g red remembered them also. Sherry and Joyce are family to the other side in more ways than one.

" Joyce sons pose to be the one changed stone, Fatts."

"No suh law." Tiwan nipped that lunacy, rumor, gossip, whatever Moe he wanted to call it, in the bud. Joyce and sherry were family.

" On chief Malik facing. The east!" dip turned his

Body east slowly. Right palm raised high; fingers extended.

Before closing his hand in to a fist bringing it to his chest with the same speed, he used to raise it to rest over his heart. The whole time never breaking eye contact with Tiwan who was standing across from him. C. Red sat cross legged in a lawn

Chair, silently taking in what the g dip was presenting to them.

"I'm not drawing Moe." Tiwan said, frowned up.

He couldn't understand where the g-dip was coming from with his deadly allegations. Dip understood They're doubt, he removed his dead son's phone from his pocket, and moved to show Tiwan the snap chat video he Screen recorded of henny wearing Fat's chain.

Next, he showed them henny snap of BH proposing to vanessa after that one. G-law could be seen smiling brightly in the den of the enemy. Tiwan shook his. Head sadly. What dip was saying could be a hundred percent accurate.

"Stone, I'm all over this. Draw, we don't need them videos leaving a trail back to us. Key 78 em Moe." Tiwan told him. Meaning. Keep them private or forget about them all together.

These were the highest throughout the other side. Right under the p. Dip knew once the three was upon agreement. Chosen ones from around the city of would be called on to strike to bring death in the name of the almighty black stone.

CHAPTER SEVENTEEN

" I am not finna be in no cast the whole summer." henny vented, swerving through traffic with her foot on the gas. Enjoying the super charged us engine.

" Crash my truck you gone be in a cast the rest of to life hoe." vanessa threatened seriously from the passenger seat of her range rover.

Vanessa was moody and short tempered. BH was Out moving around none stop since returning from them Family short vacation more than a month ago. His continued activeness in the streets terrified her.

On Top of her fear of him getting into something, she hadn't bled for nine weeks. More than a lot of sexing been going on .

"Yeah bitch. You are pregnant." Henny countered, disregarding her best friend's threat as she muscled past the other cars on the e-way.

She shook her head at what henny said. It was really No problem if she is pregnant. BH is a real man. A great father and provider to his, it was just too much going On.

Word around was the police was trying to arrest and charge BH with two murders that occurred on the same day he was shot, and his friend killed. He promised her he wouldn't kill for money again, he lied. Now the heat was on.

She contemplated getting an abortion, but would have The decency to communicate her indecisive thoughts to her Husband first and foremost. She smiled at those two words: her husband.

" Bitch you 731 - past crazy, don't know if you wanna be mad, sad happy or in love."

" Shut up hoe, I know I'm pregnant. " Vanessa said seriously.

" I know my brother happy."

" He don't know." vanessa mumbled, knowing what was coming From her friends mouth next.

" Bitch, what?!" henny did a double take. We did this shit once and got away with it. I'm not finna get killed fuckin wit y'all crazy ass."

" Ima tell him. It's different this time. Too much goofy

Stuff goin on right now tho henny, I'm not finna do this shit by myself with three kids. "Her eyes watered at the thought of losing big head and having to raise the kids on her own.

"Vanessa you always gone have me. So will my babies. Push another lil big headed ass baby out, we gone be straight."

Henny promised. This was why vanessa loved her friend. henny was the reason she reconnected with BH. He was showing up and showing out at every turn. The Sex; phenomenal, the respect; mutual and stuck there.

The love, raw and locked in. Check, check and check. BH was twenty – six yet lived a life of someone twice his age. He was collecting enough war wounds To tell a story of their own. She only wanted him to slow it down, so he'd be here on earth above the dirt. Able to tell his story to his children.

She was holding him to his word, of buying her a house out in Florida somewhere. Life in Chicago was too fast and dangerous.

Henny deposited her at her doctor's appointment. Vanessa walked in with her head held high. The first Two visits were unplanned, unprepared, and unsure for insecure reasons. Now she was walking in some one's wife. Not someone, the one. Eujean Fulton.

She checked in with registration, then waited with several other women there. After an hour of waiting and playing with her phone, her doctor appeared.

"Vanessa Fulton." she called out with a bright smile. Likewise, vanessa couldn't contain hers. This was her primary care doctor. Maxwell. She stood up from the comfortable waiting room chair and followed her doctor into her examination room.

"Congratulations. That is a very beautiful ring vanessa." Dr. Maxwell complimented sincerely. Noticing the clarity in the three-carat princess cut shined brighter than her two-carat stud.

"Thank you. Treasure's father has been here for me and the kids since finding out about her." Vanessa explained Maxwell was a beautiful older Woman of color. The dr. Who delivered both jr. And treasure. She not only knew the paternity of Both her children, the background as well. Vanessa had been seeing dr. Maxwell since she first got her period at age twelve.

"I'm genuinely you grow and develop into a beautiful young woman Vanessa. From one black woman to another, you deserve it. Much more. Let's run these tests so we shall see how far along you are. Yes, you're pregnant. It's all in your face and hips as usual." Maxwell stated, confirming that vanessa was in fact pregnant .

"Alright." Vanessa let the breath out she was holding before smiling. She wasn't surprised that doctor Maxwell knew her, specifically in this type of situation.

She removed all her clothing which was carry Prey or perish stretch fit and red bottom sneakers. She placed on a gown dr. Maxwell provided. Doctor Maxwell ran the usual diagnostic tests and finished with the ultrasound.

Vanessa was coming up on her tenth week. She Declined to know the sex of their child. If her and BH decided to keep the baby, she wanted him to be present when they found out together.

Dr. Maxwell handed her her clothes and she got Dressed, she thanked her doctor again as she was on way

She called BH. He answered as she was getting back in the truck with henny.

"Yoo! Wassup my queen?"

"We need to talk. Where you at?" She asked and was shocked at the nervousness she felt turning her stomach upside down. Or maybe I'm just hungry, she surmised.

"At my og crib."

"Ima be there in a few minutes."

"Aiight." She paused before disconnecting the call. As she was realizing they didn't tell each other they loved one another, her phone vibrated with a text message.

BH: I love your schemer 100, 100

Vanessa: I love you more BH

BH : I love you infinitely

Vanessa: and I love you more than all that, 100 100

She smiled brighter than the VVS on her ring finger.

BH was the cure to her deepest insecurities. She rarely doubted him or herself anymore. When she did, he was On point like Stephen curry to assure her that he was were She wanted him, when she needed him to be there, because its where he truly wanted to be.

If that even made any sense to anyone outside of her. Her and henny stopped on 69 and Ashland at fat Albert's Where she got them, her and BH both Italian beefs dipped in pepper oils. Henny got an order of gyro cheese fries. BH and pezzy were sitting on the stoop in front of his mother's building when vanessa nem got there.

Vanessa was already punishing her Italian beef. BH walked up on the passenger window and grabbed her

Hands as they were raising the Italian beef to her Mouth. Before she could stop him, he took a huge bite out of her food, dropping some on her windows edge.

"Big head stoppp!"she moaned as if she was in Physical pain watching what was left of her hoagie Crumble and fall out the aluminum foil and wrappings. She could cry for real. Fat Albert's was the best. BH laughed with a mouthful of her food.

"Fat bitch ass pezzy." Said about BH, shaking his head left to right.

"You wrong brother. "Henny said but was laughing with BH.

"You know what." Vanessa snapped, opening the passenger door.

BH ran behind pezzy.

"Here pezzy. You can have his shit." She Passed the bag with his Italian beef and pop in it to pezzy.

"What?" BH had a stupid look on his face.

"Damn, good looking sus. I'm hungry then ah mafucka." Pezzy Laughed as he took the bag from her hand and sat back

RAYVON PARKER   225

"TB don't play with my food Brody." BH warned seriously.

Like he was willing to fight for his Italian beef, peaky laughed at have as he started to fuck the Italian beef over like ab starved lion or some,

"Awe, you mad now?", vanessa laughed. Leaving her door open as she walked up on BH.

"Hell yeah! I'm mad. I thought you was eating without me." He Responded sounding like one of the kids, everybody laughed at him.

"Never that. But you ate yo baby piece." She said cryptically. BH looked at her through squinted eyes.

She stopped In front of him with her hands on hips and her legs Locked back effortlessly the way only someone bowlegged And pigeon toed could effectively achieve.

She was waiting on his big head ass to catch on. He did. He looked down at her stomach.

His eyes flicked down at her stomach. she nodded her head up and down.

"Ahh!" she screamed as he snatched her up with no regards for the cast on his arm and swung her around playfully excited.

"On big homie I sco every time I shoot." He joked in pezzy direction.

"You stupid. "Vanessa laughed. So Wassup? "

"Wassup? " he repeated to his self incredulously. his face got dark with anger. "fuck you mean Wassup?!"

He went from overly excited to flashing out in Seconds. The ice in his voice contradicted the fire In his eyes. She froze momentarily.

"Big head, I'm sayin are you sure you wanna do this With everything that's goin on right now?" She had recovered smoothly and made her position clear. *This crazy mafucka damn near made me pee on myself. His ass is past crazy. She thought to herself.*

"what's yo last name? He asked, softening his tone

As he wrapped his arms around her slim, thick waist with a gentleness you'd never expect. "Fulton. "she responded even softer.

"Did you hear that shit pezzy?" he asked, looking over at Pezzy who busy smashing his Italian beef. "hell Naw. " Pezzy burped, edging him on.

"what's yo last name schemer?", he asked her again, kissing her forehead.

"Fulton. " she stated a little louder staring down at her feet.

"A henny?!"he called over loudly to the open range rover.

" Huh, brother?"

" Did you hear that shit g?"

" Hear what?!" , she asked puzzled and Pezzy laughed.

"what's yo last name love?", he kissed the tip of her pretty lil nose this time. She raised her head to give him eye contact before loudly announcing.

"Mrs. Fulton mafucka!"

" We heard that." henny and pezzy said in unison and all four of them laughed.

" Schemer you my everything for real, for real, I got you

And every part of you until the end of time and ain't no such thing. Don't do that no more. Question us. Please?!"

" I'm sorry BH . I'm scared, I never thought this would be my life BH . Never. I'm not given this back to God. On my kids, none of it! We goin in the ground together nigga. Think I'm playing." vanessa pledged emotionally.

A fat tear fell Out of her left eye. Punctuating he kissed her tears away before Kissing her lips.

"We good schemer. On big homie."

"Stop Merch in stuff on him. "she said with heat, placing his hands on her stomach as she put her back to his chest.

"On my love for you and my kids, we str8."

" that's better. Now go get yo food from pezzy, she egged him on laughing

CHAPTER EIGHTEEN

Although now married and on his way to becoming rich. Father four times over, BH had been moving recklessly. he Was unintentionally neglecting home in his pursuit to Run up a real bag for his plans to exit stage left permanently as has schemer desired.

He was serving every thing Moving. Slidin on the other side and posting up on the block right where his boy while was killed. Right where he put that elephant bullet in kc.

Fuck it. he retained his own lawyer independent of the team of high price lawyers t-nator drop check on. Mike speeks, an extremely intelligent man of cover that came equipped with street sense and a hood nigga Romeeka was the source to refer him, she told big head that she used him for her last possession case and for a few of their workers. She laughed.

Telling BH to check him out and let her know .

BH, suspicious to the point of paranoia. He wasn't going Nowhere the police can box hem in for a double Murder. He let mike meet with him at his mother's apartment, when he buzzed mike in the building, he thought it was a hit.

The man had a bald head, graying goatee, Rocking a gray Nike jogging suit and wheat times. His hands were gripping a phone and car keys tight In his hoody pocket, but it gave the impression of something else entirely. Pezzy drew the monstrous FNH 57 and mike didn't even blink nor flinch.

This mafucka a steppa! BH had thought when mike bravely took a step across the threshold and into the dark hallway with two suspected killers. I like this cat. BH thought further.

Mike was locked in at that very moment. He sat Down with BH in his mother's small Living room and Told him flat out;

"fuck them, you don't have to link With them for shit dude they get a warrant, they can Call me. I did the research. Yo boys' blood was

Everywhere. Specifically, all over the gun found and Guess what. They need a witness no matter what so fuck them. Dead men say no tells."

Michael I. Speeks departed his mother's apartment With ten thousand cash. Real recognized real I suppose. Jeezy said that. The police needed BH to tell on himself. That wasn't possible.

That was three weeks past. Today was two g Birthday. He was throwing a fee fee (fiesta) out west On ridgeway and division. BH was really attending The festivities so he could get the rest of Fatts Jewelry off, two of the three chains and charms worth more than a quarter million. Ro ro had two hundred gees for him. Which He planned to use to buy a crib out in Florida. For vanessa and their kids.

Pistol and dough, with Two more of their homies riding in pistols green Challenger, followed BH and pezzy and they're homie Gerald in pezzy SRT 8 jeep Cherokee Six of them held FNH 57's. Gerald clutched A 45. IR 1911 with a forty-round drum. BH was dressed In top-of-the-line prey or perish. His shirt read:

when A woman mentions another female; she's worried. when a

Guy talks about another man; he's sorry. (a picture of the Shush emoji) the back of his straight fit jeans had prey or perish arched over the back pockets in red to accentuate the red bottom sneakers on his feet.

Pezzy wore a prey or perish outfit also. His shirt read:

Most of you got the Cinderella syndrome. (With pictures of Busted designer shoes on it) he wore identical pant as BH, except the prey or perish on the back was orange to match his Prada's Prey or perish apparel is the hottest urban clothing Line since red monkey, evisu, Pelle Pelle by marc Bucannon and true religion. No one knew who owned It. Once that it hit the world like crack cocaine in the mid 80s and frosted flakes in the early 2000 s.

Two g had the car wash on division double as a club and a parking garage for his VIP's. Earlier in the day it was a block party theme where The kids and their mothers enjoyed barbeque and Bouncy houses all through the day. Now the spacious car wash was packed to capacity

As if it were K. O. D. with two stripper poles, sitting on Top two stages the main attraction. When BH nem pulled In after calling two g, BH saw a bad ass white girl with platinum blond hair tatted from heaven to hell going bananas on one stage.

A thick caramel skin complexion , small, young looking female with tattoos all over her face dominated the other one. She

Was beautiful. Ro ro was boking heavy's out at the stage with the built white girl, throwing ones like a mal functioning aim machine.

She had on a tight little blood red dress that Could've been designed by her it fit so perfectly. some beige jimmy Choo wedges and not so subtle ice around Her neck. At nineteen, ro-ro was knocking em out. BH Walked up on her as she was dipping into an over sized Jimmy Choo bag held by a red bone that might've Been her cousin, for another roll of ones to send first class to the performers.

"That bet not be my money ro." BH capped, stopping behind her.

'If it is!?" she capped back. She was too sexy with her Brazilian inches curled to perfection.

"If it is…you more than worth it ro." He replied smoothly and she smiled.

" thought so. betta neva forget it nigga." She said cockily as she turned to give her attention Back to the white goddess. BH was about to pull her to the side. He felt Exposed standing in the open, clutching his small Gucci Bag with a nigga he killed jewelry inside. Before he could follow his thoughts, Romeeka turned to face him again.

"I ah give you a three some right now. Me, you, and this white batch, if you give me some dick." She was dead serious.

"Bet." He agreed for the sake of privacy. "let's take care that business first."

"Merch it." She tested him, BH walked away, back over to the jeep where pezzy, pistol and Gerald were lounging.

Two g walked over, and they wished him a happy g day while BH introduced pistol and the rest of his homies. BH , t-nator and big nick here, they wanna rap wit yak lick bruh. Two g told him.

"Aiight. Gerald, hold this." He gave Gerald the Gucci bag.

BH, Pezzy and pistol followed two g to the back and up the Stairs to the owner's office. T-nator, big nick, and another heavy name lo were Up there laughing like old chum. The best of friends. maybe because that's exactly what they were.

Lo was a light Skinned pretty boy with glasses, he was a known killer before he started to get that dog food money out west.

Him and big homie where super close before big homie was assassinated while pezzy and BH were on lock.

"Lil bruh, you good? ", t-nator asked as he got out his seat to show BH some love. nick and lo did the same.

"I'm breathing. What's the word tho?" BH countered with light Ice. Kc was their homie and or associate before big head was ejaculated. He wasn't really feeling none of them. Kc drew blood. For what reason? For whom?

"Yo big head ass know that shit ain't come from the round table." Lo said to BH.

"ion know shit but that my blood was spilt. Same way I still don't know what went down with my big homie."

"Shorty that was my mafuckin man's ah hunnid grand. If I knew, you'd know where they buried the mafucka responsible whole family. on Larry G! All of them bitches ah be dead! " Lo said with conviction.

"Check this out, that two B's you got from me, we straight on. I wanna see you with some. Just come shop. I love you lil niggas." this came from big nick.

Big nick was one hundred percent for the guys. He A killer but would play his position with no problem if it came down to ride. Pezzy, in BH place Had been copping blocks from nick at the same price Of thirty that he gave them to BH. T-nator was silent as usual.

"Who had the wheel for kc?" BH asked. Pistol was leaned Up against the wall behind a quiet two g. There wasn't Any tension whatsoever present inside the small office.

"The cobra felt some type of way about y'all siding wit Lil bro nem over all that money." He nodded at pistol. "You Fucked fatts up (pezzy nor pistol knew this) and kc was salty all the way around the board. his brother Luke had the wheel." Nick gave it to him straight like that.

Everyone inside that room knew Luke would be dead in the next day or two. BH was relentless and cold blooded.

"I don't blame you for gettin put up, you smart. But I'm not gone act like I understand you not reaching out to me either, we back tho, right?" this was t-nator.

BH was ninety - five percent positive that tnator Was clear from the get-go. It was his heavy weight Association with king cobra that paused their relationship. Like we never left big bruh, BH assured him. They embraced with a shake and half hug.

"Yeah! I love you lil bad mafuckas. I taught y'all a lot of that shit." Lo said shaking up with them also.

Pezzy and BH introduced pistol. Nick told folks that If he was there with them at that moment, he wasn't a homie, he was family, he offered him the bricks at thirty thousand if he was willing.

Hell yeah! Pistol told him. The seven of them went down To the party where two g climbed on top of his 71' Chevelle with a white paint bucket, dumping a boat load Of singles on top of both strippers.

It was a fuckin blizzard of dollar bills surrounding the strippers. It appeared to be fifteen to twenty thousand in singles, two g, ro ro, and their brother were checkin a lot of money on ridgeway.

While they were sippin d'usse and Poppin $30 ups' Designer ecstasy pills, ro-ro text messaged and told BH To come by the house with the jewelry, Pezzy tried to Leave out with him but he stopped him. It was only family and the guess on location, plus, he had that FNH 57 on his hip.

As he was leaving, his brother stacks pulled in in A rented white glk Benz truck, he was with his baby Mama, San San. The only one BH held any love for. She was dark chocolate and a rider for real. Both were dressed In Gucci head to toe. Stacks got out the truck and hugged big head.

"I already know big bro." He said with a wild look in his eyes.

"Fuck you been?" BH asked emotionally as he hugged his brother back tightly.

"Gettin my mind and money together. I went to the sota's

(Minnesota) wit san-san Sydney fucked my head up." BH noticed he tattooed R.I.P Sydney on the right side of his face. He took a skinny ass blunt from behind his ear, when he lit it, a funny pungent smell shocked his nose.

"Money what the fuck is that ?!" He asked taking a step back, San - San turned her nose up and stepped back herself.

"This that wet (or""-leaf) shit big bro. I done killed

So many niggas in the sota's- ",

"Chill lil bro." BH was ready to get his little brother,

Get in the car and take him home to their mother. He felt bad. Responsible. He was the one got his little brother marching in his footsteps.

"On big homie I'm str8. On Sydney grave." BH phone vibrated again with a text message from Romeeka, he told stacks money not to leave without getting Up with him first. The back of the car wash opened into The t-alley of ridgeway. BH left the t-alley and saw that no matter the extravagant party going down over at the car wash, the strip was still pumping strong.

He was dialing ro ro number as she was coming out the hose with an orange, white, and blue Audi grocery store bag that was lumpy in all the right places.

"No mgm bag this time, huh?" BH asked. stopping in front the small gate that surrounded their two flats.

"You are too ungrateful for me to keep spoiling you shorty." she Stated conceitedly.

"Ungrateful?" he laughed.

"Yeah, ungrateful. You got a new bitch so I can't even Taste this dick no more, huh?" She was in his Face. The only thing separating them is the small gate And BH loyalty to his wife, vanessa Fulton.

"I'm married ro. me and you both know I on fuck around Like that." He shot pezzy a text for them to pop out. BH had no intention to lack Tryna party with two hundred thousand on him.

They could double back once the sack was secure. Ro- ro came out the gate and pressed her body to his.

She was fronting her shit.

He reached for the Aldi bag, and she tried to kiss Him. He dodged her smoothly while simultaneously relieving her of the grocery bag full of money. Now he had the Gucci bag in one hand and the Aldi bag in the other.

Ro ro took advantage of his hands being full. She wrapped Her arms around BH waist and he hesitated. His hesitation was due to his reflex. It almost made him drop half a million dollars to get her arms off him.

"Romeeka come on g. Take this j and let me

This bread up." He was being nice. He felt like she was Rollin (high off x).

"Eujean I'm sorry! I will do whatever to get you back. That 50k was my money. I still got that watch. This 200k my money. That bitch can't do this for you." The hairs on the back of his neck stood up.

Not only for the disrespect ro was throwing at his wife. He felt danger near, he lifted his head In time to stare directly into two hates filled Eyes and a huge gun's barrel.

Boom! Boom! Boom! Boom! Boom! Boom! Boom! Boom boom!

Chapter nineteen: Vanessa

"Arrrrh!" Vanessa screamed as tears forced themselves out her eyes and down her beautiful chocolate face.

"Oh, my fuckin god., you killed them, henny cried as she sped towards the expressway.

"I hate niggas! I swear to fuckin god's I hate no good ass niggas! "Vanessa cried and screamed, waving the gun around.

She couldn't believe she was stupid enough to believe everything BH said. That she was stupid enough to marry him so fast, stupid enough to get pregnant by him. Again.

Stupid enough to give him his one plus two. To personally see him hugged up with another woman Drove her mad. Over the edge. All their people were Talking about two g party. The entire city was talking about It. This would be her last time being able to come out and have fun before she started to show. E she was four months pregnant!

Too far along for a simple abortion. It would be taking the life of her formed child to attempt to get

Rid of her baby at this stage. When they turned up Ridgeway and she saw big head and another female (Obviously not her) entangled, she asked henny who is that all on Bh?? His ex -. A shocked henny responded.

Those two words were the blasting cap to her trillion tons of dynamite. Those two words were all that played over and over in her tortured mind, twisting

Her blurred insecurities until she popped.

His ex -, the look of admiration flashing across her husband's face the day his ex-gave him fifty - thousand dollars, danced in her mind's eye. To have been through things a woman twice her age may not have been strong enough to overcome. To Survive. Made her extraordinary. To be able to open and express these Things that you fear that you feel controls you, to the one You believe will protect you from it all, takes all of you. To have that same indestructible person use your secrets, fears, troubles and nightmares against you, hurts more than it did when that same sick individual did what they did to scar you. How so? Because it is so unexpected from the warrior who happens to Be the love of your life. Because it's the love of your life, your protector and they're supposed to have your back, front, and both sides up and down no matter what.

On auto pilot, she reached over henny with a brand-new SRC 9 mm and tried to extend her arm far enough out the window to touch them both from the passenger seat of her range rover in the middle of the street.

She Warned him! While she heeded his, he disregarded hers! Now she prayed they burned in hell. Together.

Henny sped off ridgeway. Left the Westside calmly for Vanessa's getaway. The same she would have professionally done for BH.

Henny was torn. She couldn't fathom what vanessa mindlessly had committed. She had always been Quick to react, hot tempered an

Made henny race out to her and BH house in hazel crest, Illinois.

The kids were with her mother. Vanessa raced inside

Their home and packed several large suitcases with as much of her and the kids' clothes and shoes as she dared. That took three trips. Next, she cleaned all the money and drugs from the safe. Maybe close to two hundred thousand and a whole brick of cocaine.

There was two brand new guns in the safe. She collected those also. When she had the range rover thoroughly filled with their belongings. She was sweaty and wild eyed. Stuck. Her mind was drawing blanks. While her heart was finally starting to fill with pain and a tinge of regret.

Henny snapped her from her daze and asked her what was next. Vanessa told her to take her to her mother's house. She wanted to be with her kids.

Henny so desperately wanted to abandon this struggle and tell vanessa to drop her off at home.

She didn't though. Dutifully, she drove her best friend to her mother's house to be with her kids.

Vanessa's emotions were going haywire. Her adrenaline was pumping again like crazy. First, she ran the money and guns into mrs.Daniels house when they got there. This included the gun she used in her crime of passion. Then all of her and the kids' things.

"Take me home vanessa, please, this is too much for me." Henny cried hard; she saw the same thing vanessa saw. It still didn't make any sense. Probably never would.

"Alright. Let me take this last suitcase in here." Vanessa promised her.

Henny got out of the driver seat of vanessa range rover and slowly walked around to the passenger side.

Skerrt!

The white GLK Benz truck slammed to A stop beside the range rover and stacks popped at. Vanessa was dragging the suitcase out the back passenger seat on the driver's side. "Henny!!" Vanessa screamed. Attempting to alert her friend right before stacks blew her head off. literally.

Boom!

Henny was dead. Laying halfway inside the range rover. The "L" (wet) had stacks standing over her, Shooting her repeatedly. Unarmed, vanessa turned to run Up her mother's front porch as stacks turned his gun on her.

TO BE CONTINUED...

WAR LOVE 2: IRREPABLE